THE GIANTS OF CYCLING

Original title: *Les Géants du Cyclisme*
© 2001 Copyright Studio, Paris, France
© 2002 VeloPress, Boulder, Colorado, USA, for the American edition
Translation: Mary Catherine Maxwell and John Wilcockson

Printed in Spain

10 9 8 7 6 5 4 3 2 1

Distributed in the United States and Canada by Publishers Group West

International Standard Book Number: 1-931382-18-2

Library of Congress Cataloging-in-Publication Data

Ollivier, Jean Paul, 1944–
[Géants du cyclisme. English]
The giants of cycling / Jean-Paul Ollivier.
p. cm.
Includes index.
ISBN 1-931382-18-2
1. Cyclists—Biography—Anecdotes. 2. Bicycle racing—History—20th century—Anecdotes. I. Title.

GV1051.A1 O5513 2002
796.6'092'2—dc21   2002066366

VeloPress
1830 North 55th Street
Boulder, Colorado 80301-2700
303/440-0601; Fax 303/444-6788; E-mail velopress@7dogs.com

To purchase additional copies of this book or other VeloPress books, call 800/234-8356 or visit us on the Web at www.velopress.com.

THE GIANTS OF CYCLING

Jean-Paul Ollivier

VELO
press®

Boulder, Colorado USA

Contents

■ The Winged Gods   118

■ The Classics   140

■ Index   190

*Climbing the Puy de Dôme in 1964, the fratricidal duel
between Anquetil and Poulidor attained new heights.
The legend was in the making, and this photo
will remain imprinted in our minds forever.*

Following a Dream

"From Bordeaux to Bayonne, I am surprised to find myself in this caravan that ruffles the girls' hair, lifts the priests' cassocks, petrifies the police, and transforms palaces into press rooms, rather than among these small boys overwhelmed with admiration and running on caffeine. I can say that my only regret is not seeing myself pass by."

It was the 1950s, and the French novelist Antoine Blondin had just discovered the Tour de France from the inside. Its hold over him would last for the rest of his life. With a gift for writing and a certain sensitivity, Blondin would inspire generations of readers, race followers, and journalists. All would feel uplifted, as if to better emulate this rare bird whose moods were certainly volatile but who always held the racers close to his heart—especially those named Anquetil, Merckx, and Hinault. Confronted with these giants of the road, Blondin had the eyes of a child bringing his dream to life.

This dream is also our own and always will be. As we prepared this work for publication, selecting in an undeniably arbitrary manner the best cyclists of the past century, we retained a thought for all the others we have loved and admired at one time or another, during a sprint or a climb, whom we have had to leave by the wayside—in the margin of an album that by definition could not be exhaustive.

This is the difficulty of the this type of book: first to choose the racers; then to classify them according to their achievements, personalities, and specialties; and finally to briefly convey their journeys, their souls, and the path that each has imprinted forever on the road and in the history books.

In this work we have created six categories, placing each racer under a particular banner. We begin with the legends—those of unparalleled abilities whose names alone invoke all the greatness, the virtues, and most of all the incredible popularity of the bicycle around the world and through the ages. The names of Anquetil, Bobet, Coppi, Merckx,

Indurain, and Hinault are inscribed forever in all of us, young and less young, as is that of Poulidor—not for what he won but certainly for the faith, the vitality, and the sense of duty that captured all of France. For Poulidor, nothing was impossible, not even a smile in the face of defeat!

With the early-twentieth-century racers, we wanted to explore the paths of cycling's great history. Here we leap back to the cobblestones of long ago, to a time when emotions surged on the roadside—fans in berets, overwhelmed at the sight of the slaves of roads in disrepair, with their beautiful mud-black faces and froglike thighs. Go Robic! There was no television to dissect the day's events—only radio reporters to make fans dream and the printed press to make sense of things.

And the sprinters? Darrigade, Van Steenbergen, Van Looy or, more recently, Kelly. Some were crazy guys and others always walked a tightrope; some were acrobats and others daredevils. In our eyes, though, they were all racing's aristocrats.

In the section we call "The Heroic Ones," we have chosen to feature those who, by their generosity in the heat of battle and courage in adversity, were able to upset the apple cart. By holding their heads high and stomping on the pedals, at the risk of losing their sanity and maybe even their lives, they contested the established order of things. Glory to Rivière, Simpson, and Ocaña, whose crashes, however painful and dramatic, have left us all a little more humble.

Of course the climbers are in this book, and justifiably so, if only to recognize their sometimes hidden nobility. Throughout time, the mystery of these winged gods has occupied the minds of technicians and inspired writers, if not mathematicians. In the dramatic setting of the mountains, where metaphor rubs shoulders with theorem, an explanation remains uncertain: How is it that Gaul, Bahamontes, Virenque, Pantani, and Herrera knew how to propel themselves more easily toward a summit than others whose ambitions explode— along with their hearts, legs, spleens, and lungs—as soon as the road rises to become a wall, a calvary? This is the mystery and grandeur of cycling.

Only the classics remain. It was necessary to bring together the racers of diverse and multifaceted talents whose common denominator was both their presence on all fronts and, through the brilliance of their actions, their ability to excel on one day or another. They too enter our cast of the Giants of Cycling.

Before him came Coppi, Bobet, and Anquetil; after him would come Hinault, Indurain, and others. But no one in the history of the sport would ever reach such completeness and demonstrate such an appetite for victory as Eddy Merckx, the twentieth century's king of cycling.

THE LEGENDS

There's a common link that connects Jacques Anquetil, Eddy Merckx, Bernard Hinault, and Miguel Indurain, a link of history that carries both a name, the Tour de France, and the color yellow. These four racers triumphed five times in the most demanding, most popular, and most sought-after cycling event in existence. Despite different styles and diverse strategies, according to the character and temperament of each— Merckx was as aggressive as Anquetil was calculating, Hinault as impassioned as Indurain was impassive—they remain bound together. Is the racer yet born who will win the Tour six times? And where is the rider hiding who, like Fausto Coppi in his time, will merge his body with his bicycle to the point that we no longer know which one is in command? Deep in Brittany, the land of cycling, could there be a rising champion whose name would come to inspire as much passion, as many smiles, as much honor and valor as that of Louison Bobet in his heyday? The fact remains that we must have infinite patience with human time and history if we hope to find another phenomenon like Raymond Poulidor, who was loved, even worshiped, for the simple fact that he sat on a bicycle saddle, sometimes winning and so often losing…. "Poupou" was the only racer among the legends to make defeat so wonderful.

Jacques
Anquetil
Perpetual Defiance

There are some men who may serve as models for young cyclists, but Jacques Anquetil is certainly not the first to come to mind. This native of Normandy never did things like other people. He raced in defiance of the laws of diet, balance, sleep, and reason. Anquetil was an exceptional character who defied all analysis.

He attached relatively little importance to his palmarès. His optimism was unbending, his ambitions strictly tied to his material

needs. This Frenchman was no Don Quixote. He practiced his profession the way he wanted, according to his own best interests, regardless of the opinions of his peers. His nature led him to sacrifice the glorious uncertainty of sport to the demands of a strict regimen established according to his own particular gifts. His pride sometimes led him to take on unusual challenges and to achieve, almost against his wishes, exceptional feats. But he fought against such temptations.

Anquetil's harmonious style, a mix of strength and agility, made one want to hop on a bike. But because his efforts seemed too perfect, the public turned away from him somewhat, believing that his victories were premeditated. He was accused of lacking panache; he retorted that he was racing to earn a living, not to lose it by unnecessary efforts.

In 1957 Jacques Anquetil took his first victory in the Tour de France. His win was unexpected because he hadn't even planned to participate in the race. The young Anquetil's chance to ride the Tour was precipitated by Louison Bobet's withdrawal from the French national team, a decision that Bobet made in the grip of a severe moral crisis at the Giro d'Italia. When he pulled out of the Tour team, Bobet never suspected that he was opening the door to a new generation, and particularly to Jacques Anquetil. Then twenty-three, Anquetil lacked experience but held solid references: good health, extraordinary endurance, climbing skills that allowed him to limit the damage done by the uphill specialists, and an indisputable talent as a time trialist.

Anquetil's time-trial skills bordered on perfection. He won nearly every time trial he rode, including the prestigious Grand Prix des Nations, which he won nine times out of nine. We must also mention the world hour record of 46.159 kilometers that he set in 1956 on the Vigorelli track in Milan.

Though he was a five-time winner of the Tour de France, history remembers his 1964 *Grande Boucle* as the summit of his success, for this was the race in which the Anquetil-Poulidor rivalry reached its greatest intensity. That year Anquetil almost lost the Tour because of overeating; he allowed himself to consume a spit-roasted lamb on the rest day in Andorra. Forewarned, Poulidor attacked the next morning from the start, taking off with the Spaniards just as his adversary was suffering through one

A solid climber, an incomparable time trialist, and endowed with exceptional endurance, Anquetil was the archetype of the complete racer.

of the worst weak spots of his career. By the summit of the Envalira Pass Poulidor had racked up a lead of almost four minutes over Anquetil. In the descent the Norman chased like a kamikaze and passed some thirty riders.

At the mouth of the valley, where the plain began, he took a short breather, then, completely revived, caught up to the leaders about 30 kilometers from the finish. The Tour was not over yet. Another memorable battle unfolded on the steep slopes of the Puy de Dôme. The image of these two rivals riding shoulder to shoulder will remain with us forever. Anquetil was at the end of his tether, but Poulidor did not dare attack him for fear of a sudden counterattack. However, when Poulidor became aware of his opponent's state of exhaustion, he finally struck, taking 42 seconds from Anquetil. This gain was not quite enough for Poupou to take the lead, though, and during the last time-trial stage of the Tour he conceded another 21 seconds to Anquetil—who won the event with a 55-second lead over Poulidor.

But wasn't Master Jacques's greatest defiance the one set up by his team director Raphaël Geminiani that allowed him to win the Dauphiné Libéré stage race and the Bordeaux-Paris classic almost without interruption? It was a crazy, insane bet that, through his physical gifts and powers of recuperation, he alone was in a position to win. After some 2,500 kilometers in nine days, he had barely an hour of rest on a chartered plane between the finish of the Dauphiné in the Alps and the start of the great marathon of the road in Bordeaux. Then came nearly fifteen more hours in the saddle. A hundred times during a dark, nightmarish night in the rain and the cold, he pushed back the temptation to give it all up, to end this terrible suffering....

But at the end of the 557-kilometer race, he battled to victory. That final ovation, that fervor of a crowd finally united with him. In his car, leaving the Parc des Princes stadium after the finish, with his wife, Janine, at the wheel, Jacques the tough guy did not hold back his tears. For the first time in his career, he cried.

Yellow became Anquetil so well that it was almost painful to see him riding in other colors.

JACQUES ANQUETIL

Born: January 8, 1934, at Mont-Saint-Aignan (Seine-Maritime), France
Died: November 18, 1987
Palmarès: Tour de France 1957, 1961, 1962, 1963, and 1964. Giro d'Italia 1960 and 1964. Bordeaux-Paris 1965. Liège-Bastogne-Liège 1966. Paris-Nice 1957, 1961, 1963, 1965, and 1966. Dauphiné Libéré 1963 and 1965. Grand Prix des Nations 1953, 1954, 1955, 1956, 1957, 1958, 1961, 1965, and 1966. World Hour Record 1956 (46.159 km).

Louison
Bobet
So Extraordinarily Proud

Bobet loved the glory and the diamondlike radiance of the spotlight. Since the earliest days of his childhood he had hoped and prayed for the chance to make his name known. On August 23, 1944, American troops passed through his hometown of Saint-Méen-le-Grand in Brittany. Nineteen-year-old Louison Bobet was there, and General Patton, riding imperiously by in his caravan, immediately drew his admiration. The young Bobet, then a baker, had found his direction. His destiny led him to follow the troops as they liberated France from German occupation. Military officials were worried to see this young man and a few others join them without training, when danger was still rampant, but Bobet fared well. On reaching Rennes he enlisted in the Forty-first Infantry Regiment. It seemed that he had a strong sense of duty to match his desire for glory.

Fifteen years later Louison Bobet had achieved a highly prestigious career on his bike and built an incomparable palmarès. The public still called for him. For that reason, he could not let go of the limelight. Louison was nearing the end of his athletic life, but he still insisted on continuing. At the 1959 Tour de France he was feeling dreadfully weak, but to retain the respect of the public he propelled himself to the top of the Iseran Pass, on the highest road in Europe, before abandoning the race. He was mortified that he could not give more of himself. After climbing into a race follower's car, he said to a journalist, "Lend me your cap so that no one recognizes me. I'm ashamed to give up." Such sensibility might also be called splendor.

Bobet chose cycling as a vocation, advised by a father who was always looking to better himself. In order to help the young Louison successfully pursue his chosen career, Monsieur Bobet set out to find a masseur who, through appropriate care and advice, could help his son avoid all the possible pitfalls. He was directed to Raymond Le Bert from nearby Saint-Brieuc, who was responsible for the Rennes professional soccer team. Forewarned, Le Bert was not surprised to see the young Bobet arrive on his bike, a food bag on his back. The masseur gave him advice, warned him against certain practices, and drilled into him the benefits of a healthy diet.

Bobet began racing for Stella, a regional bike manufacturer based in Nantes, and quickly carried the team to glory during his 1947 professional debut. An unknown, he got away to win the then prestigious Boucles de la Seine race in Paris.

At the Tour de France, however, success did not come so quickly. Over the years Bobet accumulated a string of big victories: Milan–San Remo, the Tour of Lombardy, two French championships… but it wasn't until 1953 that he earned the first of his three consecutive victories in the Tour. They didn't come without setbacks. In the 1953 Tour Bobet's personal doctor traveled to Bordeaux to lance the saddle sores that were giving him a lot of pain. Bobet still managed to win with panache, just as he would in 1954 and 1955. However, his final victory—a result of his immense courage and desire—came at great cost. He had pushed his body too far, and his saddle sores remained open. He would need an operation by the end of the year. "It was an intense time," his surgeon declared. "A grave danger was threatening our champion, and for a few months, his life was in danger." The doctor removed a lump of dead flesh and had to insert 150 stitches to stop the bleeding. Several blood transfusions were also necessary.

Louison Bobet was without doubt one of the greatest perfectionists French cycling has ever known. His stately posture, his exemplary behavior at races, and the immaculate state of his equipment all demonstrated his respect for the public and for a job that had become a passion. His death at age fifty-eight came as a surprise in 1983. French sportswriter Pierre Chany wrote, "Proud from birth, both arrogant and sensitive, this man chose very early to be a public figure, and, more importantly, an example for his peers. This ambition quickly drove him to the outer margin of the norm, with all that this unique premise entails—sacrifice, self-denial, and private satisfaction paid for dearly."

LOUISON BOBET

Born: March 12, 1925, in Saint-Méen-le-Grand, France
Died: March 13, 1983
Palmarès: World Championship 1954. Tour de France 1953, 1954, and 1955. Paris-Roubaix 1956. Tour of Flanders 1955. Milan–San Remo 1951. Tour of Lombardy 1951. Bordeaux-Paris 1959. Dauphiné Libéré 1955. Grand Prix des Nations 1952.

On the Ventoux (above), at the finish of Paris–Côte d'Azur (opposite page), and in Milan–San Remo (double page following), Bobet stands out as the image of French cycling.

Fausto
Coppi
The Tragedy of Glory

When Coppi began his cycling career, he brought to the sport all the qualities it was lacking. Technique suddenly leapt forward, and sports nutrition advanced by ten years. The Italian champion brought new dimensions to cycling, sometimes modifying the accepted norms, and carried the sport from guesswork to a scientific order.

In a 1953 work titled *The Tour at 50 Years,* this description appeared, in keeping with Coppi's status of *campionissimo:* "He is the exceptional champion. His natural gifts—such as his genuinely stupefying abilities as a climber and time trialist—are considerable, and his superior techniques of preparation, his moral virtue, his modesty in triumph and his nobility in defeat all combine to make him the number one racer of modern cycling. He has instituted a method, a genuine science of the bicycle, from which current champions draw inspiration. This Italian is an ambitious competitor who keeps a cool head. He is characterized as a high-strung racer, whose tendency to flare up is tempered by the combined effects of intelligence and willpower."

How can we explain how this humble country boy from Castellania—a minuscule village between Liguria and Piedmont—was able to single-handedly bring about such sweeping change? Coppi was tall, with a short, curiously cylindrical chest and disproportionately long legs. He was considered puny and angular, and his large eyes dominated a pale, emaciated face. Beneath this unusual exterior was the ultimate cycling organism: a slow-pulsed cardiac rhythm, a lung capacity of seven liters, and powerful adrenal glands.

His parents were simple land-working folk who counted on their children to lend a hand as soon as possible. But Fausto left the land early, at age thirteen. One day he simply planted his pickaxe in the rugged earth of the Piedmont, looked his father in the eye, and told him, "Papa, I won't hoe anymore." He then began working for a sausage butcher and delivered orders by bike. The bike! It entered normally enough into his life, as for most people at that age.

As for his racing career, it took off after he took part in the single-day Tour of Piedmont in 1939. Gino Bartali, then Italian cycling's superstar, spotted Coppi and offered him a job as a *gregario* on his Team Legnano. But the student soon surpassed the master: Coppi won the 1940 Giro d'Italia, even though World War II had started and he was serving in the Thirty-eighth Infantry Regiment in Tortona. Two years later, between two air-raid alerts, Coppi broke the world hour record at the Vigorelli track in Milan. By March 1943 he was on the front lines and within a month was taken prisoner by the Allies in Tunisia.

At the end of the war, the rivalry between Coppi and Bartali became fully developed. The two men had become relentless adversaries. The "Coppi-ites" and the "Bartali-ites" had a tremendous time. From the finish of the 1947 Giro, we remember this gripping image: two brigades of police armed with clubs—one for Bartali, the other for Coppi. The barricades

*Fausto Coppi inaugurated and then embodied
the spirit of modern cycling.*

cracked under the pressure of the crowds, and the two stars' hotels, in spite of an impressive shield of security guards, were put under siege. In 1949, his first year in the Tour de France, Coppi crushed the competition, including Bartali, and finished with an 11-minute lead over his rival. He could easily have doubled the gap, but out of respect for Bartali, he did not draw it out. Coppi possessed great sensitivity. He became "the incomparable." In the 1952 Tour de France, the organizers were forced to increase the value of the second-place prize in order to enhance interest in a race outrageously dominated by one man. A man who was about to change his life. Until that time Coppi had been overwhelmed by a persistent sadness in his home life. He felt that he had never received the love and support he wanted from his wife, Bruna. Then he found these attributes in Giulia, a doctor's wife from Naples with eyes of fire—the notorious White Lady. When Fausto became the 1953 world road champion at the end of a scorching August day in Lugano, he met his "lady" on the VIP stand. The photographers ate up the scandal and bombarded the adulterous couple with their flashes, scandalizing a prudish Italy that, in accordance with its civil and religious laws, proceeded to banish the champion and his companion from society. To escape this unhappiness, Coppi accepted an invitation to travel to the Upper Volta in West Africa with French racers Raphaël Geminiani, Henry Anglade, Roger Hassenforder, Roger Rivière, and Jacques Anquetil. Upon his return, he felt feverish. Coppi had contracted malaria. The disease was fatal. Due to his death at age forty, Coppi never lost any of his glory or endured the insult of growing old.

FAUSTO COPPI

Born: September 15, 1919, in Castellania, Italy
Died: January 2, 1960
Palmarès: World Championship 1953. Tour de France 1949 and 1952. Giro d'Italia 1940, 1947, 1949, 1952, and 1953. Milan–San Remo 1946, 1948, and 1949. Tour of Lombardy 1946, 1947, 1948, 1949, and 1954. Paris-Roubaix 1950. Flèche Wallonne 1950. Grand Prix des Nations 1946 and 1947. World Hour Record 1942 (45.848 km).

In the early 1950s Coppi became "the incomparable," the campionissimo. He is seen opposite leading an attack at the Tour of Lombardy classic.

Bernard
Hinault
The Magnificent Badger

We remember his last ride, his farewell to cycling at age thirty-two as he crossed the less-than-straight finish line drawn in the mud of a cyclo-cross race in his hometown of Le Quessoy. In the tumult of cheers and pats on the back, friendly and false alike, he ended one chapter of his life. "This is the champagne of happiness," he said as he sprayed the crowd, adding, "It's over, all over," and other words, mumbled and certainly his own, that he repeated again and again, like a nursery rhyme chanted by a child. No doubt he was remembering what he had said when he was a junior racer at the start of a local race: "Tonight I will carry the winner's bouquet to my mother!" And he did.

The public discovered Bernard Hinault in 1977. That spring in Belgium, he won the Ghent-Wevelgem classic in a solo break and then three days later won again at the even bigger Liège-Bastogne-Liège. This double triumph made him an instant inductee into cycling's hall of fame. We knew from that day on that there was a little Frenchman from Brittany—rebellious, obstinate, and above all uninhibited—who was capable of dominating the international classics. At the dawn of the 1978 season the cycling world was expecting great things from Hinault. As preparation for the Tour de France, he competed in the Vuelta a España—then held in

Bernard Hinault,
a champion of courage and perseverance.

the spring. Assignment completed. He had won his first grand tour. Several days before the start of the Tour itself, he won the French championship on a hilly course at Sarrebourg. He said he was ready. The Tour began in the Netherlands, and Hinault provided a spectacle from

start to finish. He dominated the first time trial at Sainte-Foy-la-Grande, despite the considerable opposition of Belgium's Joseph Bruyère (then wearing the yellow jersey), Freddy Maertens, Michel Pollentier, and Dutchman Joop Zoetemelk. Hinault rode with the best in the Pyrenees, where he showed that he could sustain a high rhythm on the climbs.

The next key stage was a 52.5-kilometer time trial from Superbesse to the ultrasteep slopes of the Puy de Dôme. Hinault had some problems on the climb and lost a minute to Pollentier and almost two minutes to stage winner Zoetemelk. Pollentier seemed poised to win the Tour. Indeed, on the Alpe d'Huez he managed to outdistance Hinault and Zoetemelk by a few seconds and took possession of the *maillot jaune*. But Pollentier cheated at the post-stage drug control and was thrown out of the race. Zoetemelk became the new race leader … until Hinault cut him down at the Metz-to-Nancy time trial, defeating the Dutchman by more than four minutes. Hinault had won his first Tour de France in impressive style. This was the first of a long series of victories. In 1979 Hinault won the

Flèche Wallonne classic and Dauphiné Libéré stage race and so was the odds-on favorite to win a second Tour de France. That year's highlight was the Hinault-Zoetemelk rivalry, which took on a distinct grandeur as we watched the two men arrive alone on the Champs-Élysées. Hinault won this final stage (to make a total of seven for the race); he took the green jersey as the points winner and duly took the Tour after wearing the *maillot jaune* for sixteen days. As if to rub in his superiority, his Renault squad took the team title.

Hinault's progression briefly halted in 1980. After adding complementing his palmarès with a beautiful win at the Giro d'Italia, he developed tendinitis in his right knee during a very rainy Tour de France and had to quit before reaching the mountains.

At the end of the season, though, he dramatically reversed his fate when he won the world championship at Sallanches. The race unfolded with a rare simplicity—by elimination. There were 107 competitors at the start, only 15 at the finish. The damage was done by the formidable

Domancy hill, which had to be climbed twenty times. On the thirteenth lap, Hinault began his acceleration. From that point on, we witnessed the defeat of an army in full retreat. Only the Italian Gibi Baronchelli managed to cling to the Frenchman's wheel until the final lap. Then, on the last climb, Hinault dropped his rival and took off solo toward the supreme triumph.

"The Badger"—a nickname given to Hinault by a fellow racer—added two more wins at the Giro, each time leaving the Italians in the dust. On August 2, 1983, Hinault underwent surgery on his notorious right knee. His fans wondered if he could return to his previous heights. He struggled at first but then, in 1985, capped an amazing comeback by winning the Tour de France for a fifth time. He promised then that he would return to the Tour to help his teammate Greg LeMond to victory. Hinault carried out his plan to the letter, and the French regarded him as the 1986 Tour's moral victor. With fantastic solo rides in this his final Tour, he created an unbelievable intensity, emotion, and a massive reversal of fortune. Hinault was a great champion. He reminded us of Merckx with his taste for the spectacular and by not leaving anything unfinished. Even when he

was critical of an event because of its dangerous roads—Paris-Roubaix, for example—he endeavored to win it so that he could not be accused of holding a grudge. He was stubborn—hardheaded like any true native of Brittany—but those qualities, laced with panache, only further endeared him to us.

BERNARD HINAULT

Born: November 14, 1954, in Yffiniac (Côtes-d'Armor), France
Palmarès: World Championship 1980. Tour de France 1978, 1979, 1981, 1982, and 1985. Giro d'Italia 1980, 1982, and 1985. Vuelta a España 1978 and 1983. Liège-Bastogne-Liège 1977 and 1980. Flèche Wallonne 1979 and 1983. Tour of Lombardy 1979 and 1984. Paris-Roubaix 1981. Grand Prix des Nations 1977, 1978, 1979, 1982, and 1984.

One of Hinault's greatest exploits was his solo victory at the 1980 Liège-Bastogne-Liège, raced in apocalyptic conditions (below). In 1986 he helped his teammate LeMond win the Tour de France (left page).

Miguel
Indurain
Spain's Greatest

Miguel Indurain always maintained the same elegance, discretion, and tranquillity. Success didn't go to his head. He remained calm, patient, imperturbable, private little Miguel—the Miguelito who first rode a bike at age eleven—all the way to the day he announced his retirement from racing, January 2, 1997. His progress was always steady thanks to a fairy godfather who watched over him: José Miguel Echavarri. This former pro racer was the respected and admired *directeur sportif* of the Reynolds cycling team.

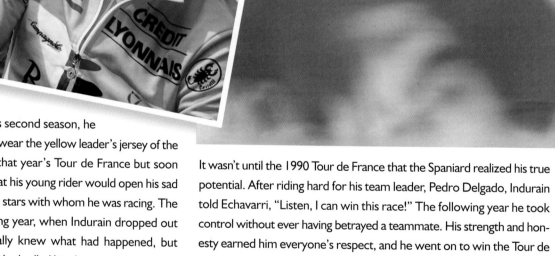

The local cycling club officials saw a champion's talent in Indurain and placed him in Echavarri's fatherlike control. Honoring the trust of the villagers, Echavarri guarded and guided the young prodigy with meticulous care. After becoming the amateur champion of Spain, Miguel turned professional in 1984 at age twenty. It did not take Indurain long to accomplish his first feat in the sport. In his second season, he became the youngest-ever rider to wear the yellow leader's jersey of the Vuelta a España. He even started that year's Tour de France but soon pulled out. Echavarri's hope was that his young rider would open his sad eyes wide enough to learn from the stars with whom he was racing. The scenario was the same the following year, when Indurain dropped out before the Pyrenees. No one really knew what had happened, but Miguel later explained that his father had called him home to work on the farm. Actually, Echavarri had wanted him to complete just the first twelve stages, but Miguel had felt fine and didn't want to quit. In order to avert any sudden action, the *directeur sportif* called Indurain's father to come immediately. Young Miguel was in pajamas when his dad appeared: "Let's go," he told his son, "I need you for the harvest." Miguel dressed in a hurry, gathered his things, and returned home to Villava.

It wasn't until the 1990 Tour de France that the Spaniard realized his true potential. After riding hard for his team leader, Pedro Delgado, Indurain told Echavarri, "Listen, I can win this race!" The following year he took control without ever having betrayed a teammate. His strength and honesty earned him everyone's respect, and he went on to win the Tour de France five consecutive times, from 1991 to 1995.

The first year it all came to a head in the second mountain stage, in the Pyrenees, between Jaca and Val Louron. That day, after attacking on the long descent from the Tourmalet, he decided to let Chiappucci catch up in the valley. At the finish Indurain took the first *maillot jaune* of his career. In 1992 he raced a phenomenal time trial in Luxembourg to wrap up victory before the Alps. In 1993 he kept Tony Rominger in

check despite a severe case of the flu. In 1994 he dominated again in the time trials, especially the one at Bergerac, where he took a two-minute lead over Rominger. Finally, in 1995, in the Charleroi-Liège stage, he executed a perfect attack that was as unpredictable as it was efficient. This last winning Tour proved to be a model of well-controlled power, intelligence, and authority. Not a single tactical error, not one fruitless effort. A near-perfect Tour.

As if in an allusion to destiny, Indurain experienced his cruelest defeat in 1996, on the day the Tour arrived in his hometown of Pamplona. But emotions were running so high that he knew on that day that the crowds worshiped him not just because he won races—they simply loved him.

Indurain was the ultimate time trial racer: powerful, lucid, relentless. In the 1986 Tour de l'Avenir, on the mythical Izoard Pass, Indurain raced toward the summit. He went on to win this under–twenty-five version of the Tour de France, taking a first step toward future glory (double page following).

MIGUEL INDURAIN

Born: July 16, 1964, in Villava, Spain
Palmarès: Tour de France 1991, 1992, 1993, 1994, and 1995. Giro d'Italia 1992 and 1993. Dauphiné Libéré 1995. Tour de l'Avenir 1986. Critérium International 1989. Clasica San Sebastian 1990. World Time Trial Championship 1995. Olympic Time Trial 1996. World Hour Record 1994 (53.040 km).

Eddy
Merckx
The Cannibal

"There was Merckx, and there were … the others." How many times have we heard this affirmation thrown out with admiration, but sometimes with irritation or exasperation, by race followers and frustrated adversaries? Eddy Merckx remains, psychologically as much as athletically, the most extraordinary phenomenon in the history of cycling. He excelled in all domains, fearing neither heat nor cold, rivaling and sometimes surpassing the climbers, unafraid of any sprinter. Dominating all his adversaries, he raised cycling to the level of an exact science. No champion has ever possessed a palmarès as dazzling or complete as this extraordinary Belgian. Magnificent, vulnerable, private, he hid his anxious, tormented soul beneath a peaceful exterior. This captivating athlete—proud, indomitable, and protective of what he had—took his performances to the verge of athletic suicide.

In defeat he retained a distinct nobility, though he did not readily admit himself defeated. Beaten one day, he found the strength to return to battle the next.

Where did he get these extraordinary abilities? Many answers have been offered. Jean Van Buggenhout, his agent, gave this explanation: "Merckx was a child raised in his father's world who very early on became accustomed to living exclusively for cycling. He doesn't lack a certain appetite for being rich, this being an era when everyone knows how to count. But his everyday intentions are those of an amateur: a victory bouquet leaves him euphoric, even though he lets nothing show, and defeat makes him grit his teeth. These childlike emotions lead him to an effortless, permanent respect for the discipline of being an athlete. He trains all the time, in winter as in summer, and manages to concentrate his mind without letting the effort bring about any mental lethargy. In this regard, he's a unique case in his generation."

When he turned pro in 1965, Merckx raced on a team with the prestigious Rik Van Looy—though not under his command, which explains why their relationship lasted only a short time. The newcomer made his talents and ambitions much too obvious. He then joined the Peugeot team in France, with whom he won the first of his seven Milan–San Remo victories. By 1968, when he won his first Giro d'Italia, Merckx was racing for the Italian squad Faema. He was only twenty-three and had already won a world title, a Flèche Wallonne, and a Paris-Roubaix. Attack remained his first instinct; panache was second nature. It was time for him to try his luck at the Tour de France.

The year was 1969. In the Alps, Merckx separated himself significantly from his two main rivals, both former Tour winners, Roger Pingeon and Felice Gimondi. Merckx wasn't content with just winning the Tour, he wanted to *dominate*. On the stage from Luchon to Mourenx in the Pyrenees, he embarked on a crazy escapade. There were 140 kilometers left when he took off alone, inspired by the majestic mountain backdrop. Nothing could stop this pedaling machine. He arrived at the finish almost eight minutes ahead of the competition.

The following year he continued his rampage, stamping out all opposition. Where the wheels of his bicycle passed, the grass did not grow back, as the French say of Attila the Hun. Three times Merckx achieved the Giro-Tour double victory. He did not simply win the races—he grabbed them and walked away with them. When he decided to win, there was nothing his opponents could do. To battle Merckx they had to rely on the chance of a technical mistake. For him there were no underhanded tactics, no false statements, no contrived incidents, no weaknesses uncovered.

His proportions were a near-perfect fit with athletic ideals: a harmonious blend of muscles, a high pelvis, perfectly cadenced leg movement, a head projected forward in the fashion of a great leader—and the whole physical package served by a staggering ability to recuperate. Merckx managed to break down any notion of resistance in his opponent with the aid of unprecedented aggression. He was comfortable on any terrain: the cobblestones of the north or the straightest of roads, the long ascents in the Alps and the Pyrenees or the steepest hills, not to mention the demanding back roads of the Flemish countryside. He could get away with long solo breakaways because he dominated his opposition in time trials, conscious of his ability to sustain a prolonged effort. Some saw his insatiable appetite for victory as excessive egotism, but it is more appropriate to view his temperament and behavior as a mark of honor. His victories were not the fruit of another's labor but very much his own. His performances honor cycling and all those who love the sport.

In yellow (left page and below) or in pink ahead of Gimondi and Dancelli (double page following), Eddy Merckx could play no other role than to ride at the head of the peloton from start to finish.

EDDY MERCKX

Born: June 17, 1945, in Meensel-Kiezegem, Belgium
Palmarès: World Championship 1967, 1971, and 1974. Tour de France 1969, 1970, 1971, 1972, and 1974. Giro d'Italia 1968, 1970, 1972, 1973, and 1974. Vuelta a España 1973. Paris-Roubaix 1968, 1970, and 1973. Milan–San Remo 1966, 1967, 1969, 1971, 1972, 1975, and 1976. Tour of Lombardy 1971 and 1972. Liège-Bastogne-Liège 1969, 1971, 1972, 1973, and 1975. Tour of Flanders 1969 and 1975. Paris-Brussels 1973. Flèche Wallonne 1967, 1970, and 1972. Grand Prix des Nations 1973. World Hour Record 1972 (49.431 km).

Raymond
Poulidor
A Reflection of France

Poulidor walked straight into history, thanks to the imprint he left in the hearts of his fans. Poulidor has become almost a household name. He is the symbol of the competitor who's always defeated—or, more simply, eternal runner-up.

Raymond Poulidor was the embodiment of grassroots France. The French loved him for his human qualities, for he belonged to the real world. He was self-made, the product of hard work and determination. Nevertheless, he remains for many a perfect example of missed opportunities and, more importantly, the dreams of those bullied and defeated—misfortune overcome and revenge of the downtrodden. He was as popular as he was unlucky. *Unlucky* isn't quite the right term.

Bloody, bruised, crushed … France has never loved defeat so much as with Poulidor!

When he arrived in the peloton he came up against a well-established Jacques Anquetil. Then, as the curtain lowered on Anquetil's career, Poulidor encountered another exceptional athlete: Eddy Merckx. Poulidor often experienced bad luck in races. Never has a champion of his status spent so much time waiting on the side of the road for help from his team car or a teammate. But to most people Poulidor was first and foremost a hero, a hard worker, a good guy—a characterization that made him a celebrity. Anquetil will forever belong to the history of cycling, thanks to his remarkable palmarès, but the public never knew him on a first-name basis. As for Poulidor, his nickname entered into our vocabulary, and from the beginning we have familiarly referred to him as "Poupou." He could have won the Tour de France or at least worn the *maillot jaune*, but would the Poulidor phenomenon still have existed? It is perfectly reasonable to doubt it. And the legend of eternal runner-up that clung to him so tightly was reinforced when, in Anquetil's absence, Poulidor helped French teammate Roger Pingeon win the Tour. This selflessness only added to his halo of popularity.

Antonin Magne, Poulidor's *directeur sportif* for most of his career, said: "He had all the virtues of a champion, particularly in that he never made an 'arrangement' with a rider outside our Mercier team. He never

obtained his results with the cooperation of complacent opponents, for Raymond Poulidor always had the pride to make sure that his victories were his own work. He benefited from an outpouring of affection—from the public and his young fans—due to his smiling good nature, his modesty, and his constant attacking. He was the total 'fighter.' He built a reputation, as his name was destined for success, with its three syllables ringing out in the wind like a banner, a name that attained radiance as soon as it was uttered."

Poulidor gave birth to an unprecedented phenomenon that rapidly surpassed the realm of sports, dividing France in the manner of politics. Though he had already won some classics, he didn't line up for his first Tour de France until 1962, when he was twenty-six. With a broken bone in his hand, he rode most of the race in a cast, drawing respect from the crowds. More importantly, he became the discovery of that Tour, winning the Chartreuse stage between Briançon and Aix-les-Bains, placing third in the next day's time trial behind Anquetil and Ercole Baldini and finishing in third place overall. Although he failed in 1963, Poulidor gracefully entered the Tour's history books in 1964. We'll never forget the image of Anquetil and Poulidor elbow to elbow on the slopes of the Puy de Dôme.

In the 1966 Tour Poulidor was the strongest. Unfortunately, he saw rival factions unite against him once again. But he would never be more popular than he was that year, when he lost the Tour by only two minutes to Lucien Aimar—who had received a helping hand from his teammate Jacques Anquetil. But Poupou's legend continued to grow....

And continued. The Tour de France was his whole life, even though it refused to crown him. Things had not changed by 1968, when he crashed heavily on the Font Romeu-Albi stage. When he was pulled to his feet, his face covered in blood, his knee in pain, one calf swollen, he realized that he had just lost another Tour. The eternal victim.

In 1969 Eddy Merckx appeared on the scene. Poulidor's chance had passed, and he became Poupou for eternity.

If Anquetil (left) had not existed, would we have appreciated Poulidor as much as we did?

RAYMOND POULIDOR

Born: April 15, 1936 in Masbaraud-Mérignat, France

Palmarès: Vuelta a España 1964. Milan–San Remo 1961. Flèche Wallonne 1963. Paris-Nice 1972 and 1973. Dauphiné Libéré 1966 and 1969. Critérium National 1964, 1966, 1968, 1971, and 1972. Grand Prix des Nations 1963. French Championship 1961. Second in Tour de France 1964, 1965, and 1974.

CYCLISTS OF HISTORY

What could Maurice Garin, the first winner of the Tour de France, and Lance Armstrong, the most recent *maillot jaune*, have in common? Nothing and everything. The world has changed. If Garin returned to the world of the living, he would feel like a voyager in space and time. "One fine day in July," Maurice Vidal pleasantly wrote in his magazine, *Miroir du Cyclisme*, "[Garin] will be led down a French road. He will ask what everyone is waiting for, what these millions of feverishly happy people are hoping to see. Then a fellow in a cap will cry out to him: '*C'est le Tour de France, papa!*' And Garin will know which country he has entered."

The names that follow are of central importance to the history of cycling. For the most part they were considered the "slaves of the road," as Albert Londres first wrote. After the 1930s they became the first heroes of the almost modern sport of cycling, spreading lightheartedness and simple happiness in their wake. Leducq, Pélissier, Magne, Speicher, and Vietto, to name only a few of those pedaling devils, mapped out and created the roads of France just as much as the civil engineers of its Highways and Bridges authorities.

Gino
Bartali
Gino the Pious

Of all the Tour de France winners, it was unquestionably Gino Bartali who inspired the richest vocabulary and gave rise to the most flowery comparisons: the Taciturn, the Pious, the Mystic. ... He was seen in many different lights. Sometimes he was the champion of simplicity, at other times of snobbery, tolerance, or tyranny. The *tifosi* surrounded him as he passed, as if to embrace him or even just touch him.

In 1937 his reputation reverberated beyond the Alps. When he appeared at the start of the Tour de France, the crowds revered him. He scaled the mountain passes with diabolical violence, pulling permanently ahead and literally scattering his opponents. The Galibier crowned him best climber, but a crash into a riverbed the next day forced him to abandon the race and delayed his consecration.

He returned the following year. This time there was no doubt that Italy was in possession of a new *campionissimo*. He won the event. Easily. No one else could ride at his level. At Briançon, his supporters came from across the Alps, and when they prepared to carry Bartali in triumph, the president of the Italian cycling federation cried, "Don't touch him; he is a god!" By the finish in Paris the Italian was more than 20 minutes ahead of the runner-up, Belgian Félicien Vervaecke.

After Bartali's victory in the 1938 Tour, the war stole away the best years of his career, but he remained a force in cycling. Fausto Coppi, five years his junior, had already proven his talent with a Giro d'Italia victory in 1940, when he should have been no more than a water carrier for Gino. A permanent and pervasive rivalry had developed that was dividing the Italian peninsula into two factions. Coppi, the rising star, had a slight edge on Bartali, who considered this situation a major irritation. Ten years after his first victory in the Tour de France, Bartali appeared

again at the start of the *Grande Boucle*. Once again victory would be his—a feat unique in the annals of Tour history.

When Bartali won this second Tour, he was thirty-four years old and had a serious case of apprehension. Of the racers he did not know, he noted which ones appeared worthy of surveillance and resolved to memorize their numbers. There were about twenty. From the start, this project was like keeping watch over a flock of sparrows. Some kilometers down the road, the peloton was caught in a violent rainstorm, so waterproof jackets concealed the numbers Bartali had been watching. Pure chance placed him in the slipstream of Brick Schotte, whom he knew from having raced with him in Belgium. The Italian stuck with the Belgian with the desperation of a drowning man ... and then defeated Schotte in the sprint to win this opening stage on the small velodrome at Trouville. So goes the true story of his start to the 1948 Tour, which went against every prediction, including Bartali's own.

At Cannes, while the Tour was observing a day of rest, a scandal erupted in Italy. The leader of the Italian Communist Party, Palmiro Togliatti was the target of an assassination attempt, and the country was threatened by fanatical upsurges. The Italian prime minister himself called Bartali on the phone. "Things aren't going well," he began. "I want to ask you one thing, Gino: Do you think you can win the Tour?"

"I am not a magician," the champion responded. "The Tour ends in Paris, and there is still more than a week left in the race."

"It's important, Gino, very important for Italy—for everyone...."

The Tuscan understood. In Italy he was a sort of hero, and if he won, he could divert the attention of his compatriots and calm the atmosphere of revolt that prevailed there.

In the Alps he flew past his rivals. Louison Bobet showed great heart, but it was not enough to fight an even battle with Bartali. The Tour ended with the victory of the Italian, and in Italy there was no more talk of revolution.

GINO BARTALI

Born: July 18, 1914, in Ponte a Emma, Italy
Died: May 5, 2000
Palmarès: Tour de France 1938 and 1948. Giro d'Italia 1936, 1937, and 1946. Tour of Switzerland 1946 and 1947. Milan–San Remo 1939, 1940, 1947, and 1950. Tour of Lombardy 1936, 1939, and 1940.

No one could touch Bartali: He was a god! (Following pages) Bartali alone with the tifosi on his way to another Giro victory.

His relations with the Tour de France proved unique. He started the race without enthusiasm in 1930, won two consecutive mountain stages at Pau and Luchon, then had to drop out after a fall. Another accident at Novi Ligure, during the 1936 Milan–San Remo, left him with a fractured femur that forced him to put an end to his career.

Born at Cittiglio in Lombardy, one of ten children, Alfredo enjoyed playing the trumpet in the village's municipal band. He also loved riding a bicycle. But his family was in need of money. So Alfredo and his brother Primo moved to France to live with their cousins in Nice. There was plenty of work on the Riviera, and lots of bike races too. The young Binda found a good balance there: four days a week at industrial design school and three days for training and racing.

In 1923 he encountered the Italian champions Costante Girardengo and Gaetano Belloni. And on the potholed road up Mont Ventoux, he left them standing. That moment was the first sign of his athletic possibilities. Binda was recognized wherever he went, always the perfect gentleman. He looked good on a bike and showed delicate handling skills that helped him avoid the rocks, thorns, and other debris that often made the roads treacherous in those times.

Though he never won the Tour de France, he took his revenge as the *directeur sportif* of the Italian national team, which he led in four triumphant campaigns: in 1948 with Gino Bartali, in 1949 and 1952 with Fausto Coppi, and in 1960 with Gastone Nencini. His great wisdom was at the root of the pact—deemed impossible until then—that united Bartali and Coppi on the same team.

Alfredo
Binda
Lessons in Style

The style and victories of Alfredo Binda place him in the ranks of the great figures of cycling. He can take pride in the fact that he alone, of all the great champions, was once paid by race organizers not to participate in their event in order to preserve the suspense that makes competition exciting. This event happened at the 1930 Giro d'Italia. Binda had already won in 1925; 1927, taking twelve of the fifteen stages; 1928, with six stages; and 1929, with eight stages. Race officials therefore begged him to stay at home, and he received as compensation a prize as big as that for winning. Binda's supremacy could not have been better highlighted. The grandeur of this star from Varese remains with us—a grandeur distinguished by other high-level victories, including his three wins in the world championship: 1927, the first one of the series, on the Nürburgring in Germany; then at Liège in 1930; and finally in 1932 on Rome's Rocca di Papa circuit.

Binda won the Giro five times, with a still-record total of forty-one stages and sixty days in the leader's pink jersey—an extraordinary record. Aside from the sheer number of his successes, he also displayed a crushing superiority, which he exhibited just as well in the sprints as on the climbs.

ALFREDO BINDA

Born: August 11, 1902, in Cittiglio, Italy
Died: July 19, 1986
Palmarès: World Championship 1927, 1930, and 1932. Giro d'Italia 1925, 1927, 1928, 1929, and 1933. Tour of Lombardy 1925, 1926, 1927, and 1931. Milan–San Remo 1929 and 1931.

Binda was perhaps the first "gentleman" in the history of cycling.

Ottavio
Bottecchia
The Mason of Friuli

Ottavio Bottecchia won only a few races in a brief career. But by becoming the first Italian to win the Tour de France, he wrote his name in gold letters in cycling history.

Racing at a time dominated by Italian greats Costante Girardengo and Alfredo Binda, Bottecchia quickly realized that there were few remaining laurels to reap in his own country. However, he did finish fifth overall at the 1923 Giro d'Italia, in which Girardengo won eight of the ten stages, with Bottecchia placing first of the individuals—riders who raced without team support. He seemed destined to have a respectable career as a *gregario*. But this mason from Friuli was ambitious. With the support of a cycling friend, he got the idea in his head to try his luck at the Tour de France.

By 1923 he was already a complete racer—a good sprinter, time trialist, and climber—and was signed up at the last minute by the Automoto team of French star Henri Pélissier. Bottecchia couldn't speak a word of French. His riding, however, spoke for him. He was a revelation: second in the first stage and winner of the second, he took the *maillot jaune* and only gave it up to his team leader on the alpine stage that crossed the Izoard Pass. He finished second overall.

Bottecchia promised to return, and the following year, 1924, he was unbeatable, bringing Italy its first Tour de France victory. He captured the yellow jersey at Le Havre, at the end of the first stage, and kept it to the finish in Paris, picking up another four stages along the way. He proved himself to be a remarkable

climber, particularly on the Tourmalet stage, where he put more than 12 minutes into his closest rival. He won the Tour de France again in 1925. Bottecchia died tragically at age thirty-two. Shortly before the start of the 1927 Tour, he was found motionless on the side of the road, a few kilometers from home, with serious head wounds. At the hospital in Gemona, his suffering lasted three days. He finally died, it was said, of meningitis. The mystery surrounding Bottecchia's accident remained unsolved for twenty years. In 1947 a local farmer confessed on his deathbed that he had once thrown a rock at a cyclist who was picking grapes on his property. But the exact circumstances of Bottecchia's brutal death have never been fully explained.

*During Bottecchia's era,
in the early twentieth century,
cycling was often a solitary exercise.*

OTTAVIO BOTTECCHIA

Born: August 1, 1894, in San Martino di Colle Umberto, Italy
Died: June 15, 1927
Palmarès: Tour de France 1924 and 1925 (second in 1923)

Eugène Christophe
The Missionary of Cycling

This champion of heroic times was a model of longevity: He raced for twenty-two years. Eugène Christophe was nicknamed "Cri-Cri," or "the Old Gaul," because of the impressive handlebar mustache he wore for much of his career. His reputation remains linked to the Tour de France, in which he competed eleven times in twenty years, between 1906 and 1925. He was the first man to wear the *maillot jaune*—yellow being chosen because it was the color of the paper used by *L'Auto*, the sports journal that ran the Tour. The distinctive jersey was created by race organizer Henri Desgrange so that the crowds could pick out the overall race leader. One particular episode made Christophe the Tour's popular hero. On July 9, 1913, on the sixth stage, Bayonne to Luchon, Cri-Cri was leading the race when he felt his fork crack as he started to descend the Tourmalet. With his bike on his shoulder, he was forced to walk down the 14-kilometer descent that separated him from the nearest blacksmith shop in Sainte-Marie-de-Campan. At the time Tour rules stipulated that the riders themselves were required to carry out all necessary repairs on their machines, with no outside help. Christophe went to work. Luckily, he had learned ironwork in vocational classes at school and had retained this knowledge well enough that he was able to rebraze the fork. The repair took four hours, under the pitiless surveillance of a race commissaire and representatives from rival teams. The unfortunate incident took away any chance he had of winning the Tour.

The same misfortune befell Christophe six years later, in 1919. On the next-to-last stage he had the race in his pocket, with the *maillot jaune* on his back and a 28-minute lead over the second-placed Belgian Firmin Lambot. Then, during this 468-kilometer Metz-to-Dunkirk stage, he crossed the slippery cobblestones on the way out of Valenciennes and fell victim to another broken fork. Once again he made the repairs by himself, in a small bike factory at Raismes. When Christophe finally arrived in Dunkirk, Lambot had run up such a big lead that Christophe had no chance to recover the jersey.

Christophe's fork betrayed him a third time, on the descent of the Galibier during the Briançon-Geneva stage of the 1922 Tour de France. But his poor position on general classification made this incident less dramatic. The Old Gaul certainly cut a tragicomic figure when he arrived at the feed zone in Saint-Michel-de-Maurienne on an antique bicycle that the parish priest of Valloire had obligingly lent him.

Though the Tour de France tends to overshadow the other parts of

Christophe's career, we should mention that he won Bordeaux-Paris in 1920 and 1921, Paris-Tours in 1920, and a hellish edition of Milan–San Remo in 1910, raced in rain and snow. He was also a seven-time champion of France in cyclo-cross.

Upon his death at age eighty-five on February 1, 1970, it was in simple and moving terms that his contemporary Antonin Magne, reflecting on what had been Christophe's life's work, concluded, "No one has served our sport as much as you. Your fine career now over, you have been a leader, an educator, a devoted propagandist. With your passing, Cri-Cri, we lose a missionary of cycling."

Eugène Christophe forged his legend one day in the Pyrenees.

EUGÈNE CHRISTOPHE

Born: January 22, 1885, in Malakoff, France
Died: February 1, 1970
Palmarès: Milan–San Remo 1910. Paris-Tours 1920. Bordeaux-Paris 1920 and 1921. Circuit de Brescia 1910.

Nicolas
Frantz
From the First to the Last Day

When we flip through the archives of the Tour de France, we note that according to the experts of the time, the twenty-second edition, in 1928, was not fought out with enough fervor to please the fans. Most accounts even conclude, a little too quickly, "It was dull!" Which, it seems, was not entirely the case. We believe that the 1928 Tour deserves a closer look.

Most evocative was the path taken by the winner, Nicolas Frantz. One cannot imagine the amount of effort, attention to detail, and dedication the great Luxembourger invested in the Tour de France, preparing exclusively, all year long, for the event that he believed would yield him the most. What did Bordeaux-Paris, Paris-Tours and Paris-Roubaix matter? *La Grande Boucle* was the sole object of his interest.

One month before the start, Frantz's name appeared in the papers after he won a couple of races—simple elements of his preparation for the great event. In contrast to other competitors who preferred to find their peak form over the course of the stages, Frantz was the man to beat right from the start. He worked relentlessly to stay in top physical condition. He never made an excessive or wasted effort; this Luxembourger was the champion of prudence. In the race he was always scanning the road surface ahead of his wheels. The result—during the 1928 Tour he punctured his tires only twice.

At the overnight stops he was careful of his health and what he ate; people called him a fanatic, but he never complained. He was obsessed by detail, to the point that he arrived at the start of the Tour with twenty-two jerseys, twenty-two pairs of socks and twenty-two pairs of shorts, one for each day of the event. He accumulated reserves of energy as one would accumulate savings. A reserved man, he was the champion of technique. His contemporaries drew inspiration from his methods.

When Frantz took his place at the start of the 1928 edition, he had already won the previous Tour. This time he was aiming for a double. More than ever, he proved his supremacy from the very start—he won the *maillot jaune* on the first stage and never gave it up. He raced for the Alcyon team, which was packed with seasoned veterans: André Leducq, Maurice Dewaele, Gaston Rebry, Félicien Vervaecke, and Joseph Mauclair.

On this Tour Frantz had just one moment of panic. It unfolded on the nineteenth stage, between Metz and Charleville, which had promised to be uneventful. The *maillot jaune* had a big lead and a solid team at his disposal and was expecting the last three stages to be a cruise. Then, at a rail crossing near Longuyon, Frantz's bike collapsed beneath him. There was total confusion in the Alcyon camp. Luckily, the *directeur sportif*, Ludovic Feuillet, managed to borrow a spare machine for the champion—a lady's bike, complete with mudguards and a rear light! Straddling this heavy mount, Frantz covered the remaining 100 kilometers at an average speed of more than 27 kilometers per hour to reach Charleville with a deficit of only 28 minutes—and to keep his yellow jersey. He became only the second rider in history—after Bottecchia, in 1924—to wear the yellow jersey from the first to the last stage.

Frantz had initially been attracted to running and soccer. But, like his older brother, he saved cent by cent until he could buy himself a bike. Working on the family farm, he first had to finish his daily chores before he could turn his thoughts to cycling. So he decided to train during his lunch hour. From the start of his racing days in 1914, he began collecting victory bouquets. His progress was stopped by the German occupation of his country, but at the war's end in 1919 he took out a license to race in the junior ranks. It was the beginning of a superb career.

Frantz was the champion of technique, fanatical and well prepared.

NICOLAS FRANTZ

Born: November 4, 1899, in Mamer, Luxembourg
Died: November 8, 1985
Palmarès: Tour de France 1927 and 1928. Paris-Brussels 1927. Paris-Tours 1929.

Maurice
Garin
The Pioneer

Before the sport of cycling gave birth to the Tour de France in 1903, Maurice Garin was already an accomplished racer. And when he became the first winner of the prestigious *Grande Boucle,* he was elevated to the status of a living legend. He was the archetypical bike racer, and everything he did added to his grandeur and popularity.

At five feet four inches and 134 pounds, this first giant of the road was no Hercules. Born as an Italian in 1871 at Arvier, in the Aosta Valley, he spoke only French, which was then considered a sort of regional language in this remote region of northeastern Italy. He was a chimney sweep, like many other young men from his valley. Like them, he was skillful at maneuvering his brush through the chimney ducts and staying in top shape—the hallmark of that profession. Garin was later nicknamed the "Little Chimney Sweep."

In these late-Victorian times, France was in need of chimney sweeps, and according to tradition, the French-speaking Italians of the Aosta Valley emigrated to Paris and other big cities to meet the demand. The young Maurice grew up on the road, traveling all through the cities with his brothers and father. They made their home at Lens, a coal-mining village in northern France. The Little Chimney Sweep could do anything with his hands, so an Italian friend who had lived in Lens for a few years helped him get a job at a construction company that was looking for masons.

Garin's fierce will bordered on stubbornness, and, intrigued by the exploits of the first cyclists, he managed to acquire his own bicycle just before his twentieth birthday. Success soon followed.

When the Tour de France was launched, Garin—by then a naturalized Frenchman—figured among the most prominent racers. He was even tipped as a possible winner.

It took just one day for him to justify his ranking as he easily won the marathon opening stage from Paris to Lyon. Garin kept the lead from start to finish, and, to emphasize his superiority, he won the last two stages: Bordeaux to Nantes and Nantes to Ville-d'Avray, the Paris suburb where the first Tour de France ended. Dominating the race, Garin covered the 2,428 kilometers in 94 hours, 33 minutes, at an average speed of 25.288 kilometers per hour—leaving his closest opponent, Lucien Pothier, almost three hours behind him. The little Garin, stocky, hot-tempered, crafty, calculating, and very sharp beneath his somewhat rustic exterior, was a true phenomenon of resistance and vitality.

Crowned with this brilliant victory, Garin's career continued to blossom. He began the 1904 Tour as he had started it the year before, by winning the first stage. But the Little Chimney Sweep, though he went on to win the race for a second time, did not figure in the final results. Four months after the finish, the Union Vélocipédique de France, taking into account multiple incidents that had tarnished the event, decided to disqualify Garin and the next three finishers. The Little Chimney Sweep was never again seen at the start of the Tour. He retired with his winnings to Lens and opened a garage on the Rue de Lille. He passed away on February 18, 1957, at the age of eighty-six.

Maurice Garin, the Little Chimney Sweep, won the first Tour de France in 1903.

MAURICE GARIN

Born: March 23, 1871, in Arvier, Italy
Died: February 18, 1957
Palmarès: Tour de France 1903. Paris-Brest-Paris 1901. Paris-Roubaix 1897 and 1898. 24 Hours of Paris 1895.

and thighs made for time trialing as much as sprinting. He would dominate cycling in the period between the two world wars. Girardengo's most sensational victory came in the 1924 Grand Prix Wolber—then the unofficial world championship—in which, on the Parc des Princes track in Paris, he succeeded in out-sprinting the great Henri Pélissier and the Belgian Félix Sellier at the end of a grueling race. Though he won the Giro d'Italia just twice, he collected no fewer than thirty stage wins! His event of choice remained the Italian national championship, which he won nine times. And he took Milan–San Remo six times—forty years before Eddy Merckx began his string of seven victories in Italy's most famed classic. Girardengo was a national hero, a demigod. It was even decreed that main-line express trains would begin stopping at the small station in his hometown of Novi Ligure, an honor previously reserved exclusively for monarchs and heads of state.

Costante
Girardengo
The First Campionissimo

Costante Girardengo was the first Italian to be awarded the title of *campionissimo,* and at the time it seemed that no one but he was worthy of it. He owed this stature to his stunning career, which he began very young and with immediate success. At the age of nineteen he turned pro after taking second place in a terribly rough-and-tough edition of the Tour of Tuscany classic. His twenty-four seasons were exceptionally rich in successes of every genre and on all types of terrain. The proportion of his victories, compared to his total number of races, remains mind-boggling. Almost unbeatable in the sprint, Girardengo was an even better time trialist and climber, fearing no one. His extraordinarily sharp tactical sense allowed him to extract himself from the most complicated situations, sometimes with lots of nerve and not much in the way of scruples. Girardengo—nicknamed "the Dwarf of Novi"—had the face of a weasel, both kind and cunning. His harmonious torso ended in a solid lower back

He raced until the age of forty-three, devoting the last part of his career to the track while still remaining successful. Nevertheless, on the road he had trouble matching the young Alfredo Binda. His presence at the races was no more than a token, though he still had great prestige. When he managed to win one last victory—alone, detached, in a secondary event—the fans bowed as he passed and swept the grit off the road before he arrived. "Gira" waited on the line until the next man finished. Then, in a theatrical gesture, he handed him his bike: "Take it and look after it," he told him solemnly. "Girardengo will not need it anymore, for Girardengo will never again be seen in a race."

Girardengo was the first authentic campionissimo in cycling history.

COSTANTE GIRARDENGO

Born: March 28, 1893, in Novi Ligure, Italy
Died: February 9, 1978
Palmarès: Giro d'Italia 1919 and 1923. Tour of Lombardy 1919, 1921, and 1922. Milan–San Remo 1918, 1921, 1923, 1925, 1926, and 1928. Grand Prix Wolber 1924.

André Leducq

Go, Dédé!

The stage over the mighty Galibier in the 1930 Tour is one that is always remembered. After a fairly laborious climb, Leducq fell twice on the descent and was by then 14 minutes behind his main challengers. The *maillot jaune* seemed definitively lost. But Charles Pélissier, then captain of the French national team, told all his teammates to stop. Not only did they revive Leducq; they also paced him back to the first group. He ended up by winning the stage in a sprint at Evian and so retained the overall lead.

The 1932 Tour went much the same way. Things were looking good, favorable even, for the popular "Dédé." He totaled six stage victories and won the Tour in a manner that reflected his personality—with a smile. As in 1930, he had problems over the Galibier Pass and was in fourteenth place at the summit, three minutes behind the leaders. Again, he made a sensational comeback on the descent and won at Aix-les-Bains.

A champion with an eternal smile, the joyous Leducq had incredible morale. He viewed the toughest events with enthusiasm, motivating his teammates with good humor and impish escapades. And his serene confidence was a considerable asset. Even his last Tour in 1938—true to his character to the very end—was completed with panache. On the final stage he pulled away with his old friend Antonin Magne, and they arrived together on the Parc des Princes track to be greeted with delirium by a packed crowd. Leducq said later, "We had decided to enter as brothers. Tonin pulled to the side, I moved even with him, my right arm around his waist, his left arm across my shoulders. Both of us on the same line."

André Leducq—his was the spontaneous laugh of the good life, insolent good health and moral fortitude, and the cheeky retort without the least hint of nastiness.

Well before Poulidor, all of France was infatuated with Dédé Leducq.

André Leducq belongs to the all-time elite of international cycling. His magnificent qualities as a champion allowed him to collect great victories that became part of cycling legend.

At age seventeen he joined the Vélo-club de Levallois, a famed amateur racing team in Paris, and became a somewhat full-time student of cycling. In May 1925 Leducq enlisted in the 190th Infantry Regiment at Tours, where he was able to list the following accomplishments on his identity card: champion of France (juniors) in 1922, champion of France (seniors) in 1924 and 1925, world amateur champion in 1924, and Olympic champion in team road racing in 1924. His colonel, who advocated the use of one's abilities, ordered him to win the military championship of France, and like a good, obedient soldier, André duly complied.

Leducq quickly became a force in the professional ranks and won his first Tour de France in 1930 at age twenty-six. Powerful and sturdy at five feet nine inches and 169 pounds, he was strong on the flats and managed to hold his own on the mountain passes; in the sprint he could beat most riders, including such fast finishers as Raffaele Di Paco, Georges Ronsse, and Georges Speicher. A great descender, Leducq specialized in comebacks after the longest ascents and sometimes won mountain stages that didn't seem to favor him.

ANDRÉ LEDUCQ

Born: February 27, 1904, in Saint-Ouen, France
Died: June 18, 1980
Palmarès: Tour de France 1930 and 1932. Paris-Roubaix 1928. Paris-Tours 1931. Paris–Le Havre 1928. Paris-Caen 1930. Critérium des As 1934.

Sylvère Maës
The Blue-Collar Racer

Sylvère Maës pedaled like a grinder, but he was as clever as could be.

Sylvère Maës was coarse and unrefined, with the nose of a boxer, the hands of a laborer, and a massive torso supported by bowed legs. When at full power, he pedaled like a pendulum, pushing down on his pedals, right-left, right-left, with all the weight of his body. Maës, born and bred in West Flanders, proved to be well balanced in every way. Observant and crafty, he burst onto the international scene in 1933, winning Paris-Roubaix by edging out fellow Belgian Félicien Vervaecke in the sprint. As his reputation grew, he was given a nickname: "the Crafty Priest."

"He pedals like a grinder," race organizer Jacques Goddet wrote in *L'Auto* at the end of the French classic. "And his body forms shocking angles in an art where circular movement should control everything. One would willingly forget this ease that ennobles the toughest labor and remember the fine coordination of the muscles in their effort."

It was the Tour de France that made Maës a celebrity. Having won stages in 1934 and 1935, he started the 1936 Tour as the heavy hitter of the Belgian national team—the famous Black Squadron. This time he rode to a brilliant victory, highlighted by a courageous, powerful style of climbing that earned him a big stage win in the Pyrenees and a lead of almost 27 minutes over runner-up Antonin Magne of France. The collective dominance of the Belgians in that Tour's four team-time-trial stages certainly strengthened Sylvère's grip on the race, but he confirmed his individual superiority at the Tour's other strategic points.

He was leading the race again in 1937 when some serious accusations were made against his team, involving the complicity of a Belgian rider from another squad. The resulting scandal was enough to prompt the withdrawal of his Belgian national team at Bordeaux, with only four days remaining.

Back at the Tour de France in 1939, Maës's Belgian teammate Edward Vissers appeared to contest his leader's dominance when he took the marathon stage across the Pyrenees in a solo break. But Maës wasn't disturbed. He knew how to wait for the right moment to catch the overall race leader, an exhausted René Vietto. On the alpine stage from Digne to Briançon, he left the Frenchman more than 17 minutes behind. Maës never doubted this outcome, and a further stage win in the individual time trial between Bonneval and Bourg-Saint-Maurice put an exclamation point on his victory.

Sylvère Maës, the blue-collar racer, was a genuine master of the Tour de France.

SYLVÈRE MAËS

Born: August 27, 1909, in Zevekote, Belgium
Died: December 5, 1966
Palmarès: Tour de France 1936 and 1939. Paris-Roubaix 1933. Circuit du Morbihan 1939.

Antonin Magne
Tonin the Wise

A magnificent figure of a man, Antonin Magne marvelously demonstrated his athletic talents and exemplary honesty throughout his racing career. His favorite saying was: "Without virtue, there is no glory." He not only respected this mantra in his public and private life; he also instilled it in the generations of athletes whom he guided and directed between 1945 and 1969 during his time as a *directeur sportif*. Louison Bobet, Rik Van Steenbergen, Fred Debruyne, Raymond Impanis, and Raymond Poulidor were his most notable protégés on the Mercier team—which turned "Tonin the Wise" into a veritable institution.

Magne always maintained, "You have to know how to last, how to economize your strength so that you are as strong at the end as at the beginning." With those words, he unlocked the secret to the Tour de France. Born in 1904 at Ytrac in central France, Magne did not exactly have a gift for cycling. He started racing at age sixteen and struggled through long years of effort and setbacks before making a name for himself. But he was never discouraged. The future was his motivation. This model of perseverance took his first victory at age twenty-three in Paris–Saint-Quentin. The following year, 1927, he won another important one-day race, Paris-Limoges. And so he was slowly rewarded for his sacrifices. For having led an exemplary life, for having neglected not the slightest detail, for having constantly sought to surpass his limits, Magne accumulated an enviable palmarès before retiring on the eve of World War II. His record included, most notably, two Tour de France victories and one world championship—which he secured in 1936 after a solo breakaway on the circuit at Berne, Switzerland, finishing with a near 10-minute margin over runner-up Aldo Bini.

Soon before the start of his first victorious Tour de France, he moved into a hotel at Nay, at the foot of the Pyrenees. His arrival was surrounded with the greatest secrecy. Every other day for four weeks, he climbed the passes of the future Pau-Luchon stage, experimenting with different gears. He did not return to his farm in the Paris suburbs until two days before the start. While scouting the course, he noted that the descent of the Aubisque Pass had just been paved, with rocks left haphazardly across the entire width of the road. After several test runs on that section, he realized he would have to attack full speed on the descent in order to make the most of his knowledge. He used this strategy and won the stage in a lone escape to achieve his goal: the conquest of the *maillot jaune*. He could be characterized in a multitude of anecdotes. One is the story of how he forced himself each morning, no matter the weather, to carry a heavy rock to the end of his garden—one of the tedious tasks that he

considered a champion of his prestige should not shirk. As one who banked on sure things, he reasoned like a mathematician. His weakness, in the eyes of the journalists, was that he was not spectacular. Maybe he didn't compare well with a clown like André Leducq, or the elegant Charles Pélissier, but they spoke highly of his straightforwardness, his integrity, and his stability—products of a cool head, clear-sightedness, and a just appreciation of all things.

Antonin Magne (shown here with Sylvère Maës) had a mantra: "Without virtue, there is no glory."

ANTONIN MAGNE

Born: February 15, 1904, in Ytrac, France
Died: September 8, 1983
Palmarès: World Championship 1936. Tour de France 1931 and 1934. Grand Prix Wolber 1927. Grand Prix des Nations 1934, 1935, and 1936. Paris-Limoges 1927 and 1929. Paris–Saint-Quentin 1926. Circuit d'Auvergne 1929.

Henri, Francis, and Charles
Pélissier
Victory, Family-Style

They were the precursors of modern cycling. The three Pélissier brothers—Henri, Francis, and Charles—took meticulous care of their equipment; replaced long training sessions in the saddle with shorter, more energetic workouts; and liked races to start fast so that their opponents would be taken by surprise.

Henri, the eldest, first captured the spotlight during a brilliant campaign through Italy in 1911 and 1912, and he lost the 1914 Tour to Philippe Thys by only 1:05. After World War I he took victory after victory in the classics, to become the recognized king of international cycling. In 1923 he added the Tour de France to his collection.

Francis, the family's second son, devoted his whole career to helping his older brother—whom he called, simply, Pélissier. But this did not stop him from picking up three championships of France, two editions of Bordeaux-Paris, and the apocalyptic Paris-Tours of 1921, which only nine riders finished. At age thirty-six, he narrowly missed a third victory in Bordeaux-Paris, finishing second to Georges Ronsse. Later, when he was a *directeur sportif*, it was this race that earned him the nickname of "the Sorcerer." The youngest son, Charles, was perhaps less suited to the harsh efforts

of road racing. But, like his older brothers, he was extremely courageous, and he was smart enough to develop his own style. With an elegant appearance, he stood out from the riders of his time and set a trend by wearing leather gloves and white cotton ankle socks. He was an exceptionally talented sprinter, and he and André Leducq were the two most popular French cyclists of the 1930s.

Henri and Francis were like one person, as Francis, five years younger, had worshipped his older brothers since they were very young. Growing up in a harsh family, Francis had been terrorized, though fascinated, when he witnessed a terrible fight between Henri and their father—the family tyrant and workaholic who was solely preoccupied with the output of his forty dairy cows on the rue Mesnil, in the Sixteenth Arrondissement of Paris. Henri had dared to stand up to him, saying he wanted to become a bike racer. At age sixteen, after his father had crushed his beloved racing bike in a mighty fit of rage, Henri left the family home. Francis followed him. He too became a bike racer and blindly followed his big brother, who was calculating, bossy, and provocative. Francis was the workhorse, Henri the thoroughbred.

The rages of the elder Pélissier were legendary. He stood up spontaneously against all that represented authority in the cycling world, and particularly Henri Desgrange, director of the Tour de France. In 1924 a violent quarrel with the Tour boss led him to drop out of the race, along with Francis and Maurice Ville. On that day, June 26, the well-known journalist Albert Londres conducted an interview at the Café de la Gare in Coutances that would have huge repercussions. It was published in the

Petit Parisien journal as "The Martyrs of the Road"—a title that history would rename "The Slaves of the Road." During the interview, Henri complained about the racing conditions and the frustrations he suffered: "My name is Pélissier, not Azor," was one remark that made history. He retired from competition in 1928, becoming first a *directeur sportif* and then a trainer. It was a morose postcycling life that this highly energetic man did not tolerate well. "He was dying of boredom," Francis said. Then, tragically in 1935, Henri was killed by his mistress in what was conveniently called a crime of passion—he who all his life had been more sensitive to the desire to provoke passions rather than the urge to live them. Charles, meanwhile, just wanted to follow the path carved out by his older brothers. He possessed the character of a true Pélissier, trying to be arrogant in his own manner. But he seemed frail next to the two superstars, a contrast that led the future great filmmaker Henri Decoin to write in July 1925, "Henri and Francis are a couple of peacocks. They have fine feathers, which Charles picks off from time to time, sticks them in his back, and takes a stroll along the athletic highway like a jaybird in a peacock suit." Charles, in reality, became the antithesis of his older brothers. He was courteous and open to discussion without giving up his own fierce pride. He won sixteen stages of the Tour de France, and his popularity grew ever larger. He was, in both road and track racing, the leading young charmer, the knight of noble causes, and the invaluable lieutenant.

The Pélissier brothers at the start of the Circuit of Paris in 1922 (left page);
Henri the thoroughbred (this page).

HENRI PÉLISSIER

Born: January 22, 1889, in Paris
Died: May 1, 1935
Palmarès: Tour de France 1923 (second in 1914). Tour of Lombardy 1911, 1913, and 1920. Milan–San Remo 1912. Paris-Roubaix 1919 and 1921. Bordeaux-Paris 1919. Paris-Brussels 1920. Paris-Tours 1922.

FRANCIS PÉLISSIER

Born: June 13, 1894, in Paris
Died: February 22, 1959
Palmarès: Bordeaux-Paris 1922 and 1924. Paris-Tours 1921. Tour du Sud-Est 1920. Circuit of Provence 1920. Grand Prix Wolber 1926. French Road Championship 1921, 1923, and 1924.

CHARLES PÉLISSIER

Born: February 20, 1903, in Paris
Died: May 28, 1959
Palmarès: Paris-Arras 1925. Mont Faron Hill Climb 1927 and 1928. Critérium des As 1933. Eight stage wins at the 1930 Tour de France.

Lucien
Petit-Breton
Man of Bronze

In the cycling record books, we rarely come across the name Lucien Petit-Breton. Instead, he is often referred to as simply Petit-Breton or the Argentinean, for the childhood years he spent in Buenos Aires. He was also known as the "Man of Bronze"—so legendary was his stamina.

He began cycling in South America, and no one had heard of him before 1905, when he broke the world hour record, covering 41.110 kilometers. A fourth-place finish in the 1906 Tour de France then put him among the sport's elite, one of the masters of long-distance racing.

Petit-Breton—whose true name was Lucien Mazan—was born in Plessé, a small village in the Brittany region of France. Both energetic and elegant, he proved to be a formidable aggressor in the two Tours de France that he won. In 1907 it wasn't until four stages before the finish, after having won the previous stage in Bayonne, that he managed to move into the overall lead. He strengthened his position with a win at Nantes and finally ran out the winner ahead of Gustave Garrigou and Émile Georget.

In light of this success, Petit-Breton was considered the favorite in 1908. He lived up to the predictions. Demonstrating remarkable power and intelligence allied to strength, he literally played with his opponents. He began by watching them—Georget, Georges Passerieu, and François Faber—while making sure to stay among the candidates for victory himself. Soon Georget began to show signs of suffering, Garrigou was complaining of the cold, and Passerieu experienced a severe loss of form; Jean-Baptiste Dortignacq later collapsed under the hot sun. Petit-Breton was left with just one rival: Faber. He shadowed his rival, and, using his fine sprint, he gathered enough points to take a remarkable second victory. In total he had picked up five of the fourteen stages, compared to Faber's four.

This first Tour double in cycling history prompted Petit-Breton to retire to the Périgord region, where he became a bike dealer. But citizen Mazan missed bike racing. When this urge reached crisis point, he leapt on his bike once again and won the Tour of Catalonia, after which he took part in the Tour de France and the Giro d'Italia—where he won the fifth stage, Mondovi to Turin. The years were taking their toll on this former bellboy of the Buenos Aires Jockey Club, but he did not admit defeat. Carefully, meticulously, he nourished a genuine worship for this sport that was his passion, going so far as to carry his bike up to his bedroom each night. Like a novice, he continued to study each race with

infinite precaution, leaving no detail to chance. This strategy is what carried him to the threshold of a third victory in the Tour de France.

It was 1913 when he accomplished yet another genuine strategic race against Philippe Thys and Garrigou. He was riding with remarkable regularity, and success was in his grasp, when he crashed on the next-to-last day. Suffering from a fractured kneecap, he was forced to leave the victory to Thys.

World War I transformed Petit-Breton into Lucien Mazan, soldier second-class, cycling officer in the second division of the general staff. He died on December 20, 1917, near Troyes, the victim of an ordinary traffic accident that took place in the middle of the night about 20 kilometers behind the front lines. His car collided at high speed with the cart of a drunken farmer.

Petit-Breton, whose real name was Lucien Mazan.

LUCIEN PETIT-BRETON

Born: October 18, 1882, in Plessé, France
Died: December 20, 1917
Palmarès: Tour de France 1907 and 1908. Tour of Belgium 1908. Paris-Tours 1906. Milan–San Remo 1907. Paris-Brussels 1908. Bol d'Or 1904. World Hour Record 1905 (41.110 km).

Albéric
Schotte
The Last of the Flandrians

We know him best by the contraction of his first name: "Brick." He remains one of the most storied Belgian racers of all time. Brick Schotte was also called the "Last of the Flandrians" for his aggressive, courageous, generous racing style and for a temperament that always tended toward the offensive.

In 1939, just before his twentieth birthday, Schotte made a name for himself in France at the Circuit de l'Ouest, a stage race based in Brittany. The best professional racers of the time were there. After the fifth stage, Nantes-Lorient, Schotte was in the leader's jersey going into a designated rest day. But a storm was brewing over France. World War II was about to break out. The race never continued, and the Belgian was declared the winner.

As a result, the cycling press took a more detailed look at this young racer. Journalists discovered that he was still an independent—a semipro—one of six children from a family of small farmers. He started work at a very young age, helping his parents tend their ten acres of land. Early in life, he wanted to race bikes, like some of his friends. As a teenager he went to work at a factory in Kortrijk every day of the week, starting at five in the morning. In the afternoons he was able to concentrate on cycling. He devoted himself to it so completely that soon he knew nothing beyond his machine. By the time he was eighteen, he had never ridden on a train and never seen the ocean, close as it was. This young man simply rode his bike.

After the war Schotte turned pro and soon established himself as an excellent one-day specialist, dominating nearly all the classics: the Tour of Flanders, Paris-Tours, Paris-Brussels, and the world championship, each of which he won twice.

In 1948, after having finished second in the Tour de France behind the untouchable Gino Bartali, he was one of the favorites at the world's, just across the border in the Dutch city of Valkenburg. Schotte exploited the rivalry between the Italians Bartali and Fausto Coppi (neither of whom finished the race), and with the active support of his friend Marcel Dupont of France, he initiated the attacks in the final few laps. On the final lap he still had to contend with two Frenchmen, Lucien Teisseire and Apo Lazaridès. Teisseire had to stop with mechanical

problems. Lazaridès remained. The sprint was not the French rider's specialty, though, and Schotte won easily.

Two years later the world championship took place even closer to home, at Moorslede, in the heart of Flanders. Brick even rode his bike there the day before the race for some last-minute training. This time he had to contend with the powerful Dutchman Gerrit Schulte, who slipped into all the breakaways. But Schotte had the last word. In the final lap he threw all his remaining strength into one last attack to finish a minute ahead of the competition. He was the world champion again, this time in his own country. That evening he was driven home in a posh convertible, hailed by thousands of fans all along the route.

"Like Van Steenbergen," wrote the Belgian journalist Theo Mathy in his *History of Belgian Cycling,* "Schotte had a remarkable career that lasted a quarter of a century. He was all courage, labor, and obstinacy, when compared with the natural talents of the great Rik. A child of the earth, he remains attached to the most simple values, modest in his fame, even a bit too unassuming."

ALBÉRIC "BRICK" SCHOTTE

Born: September 7, 1919, in Kanegem, Belgium
Palmarès: World Championship 1948 and 1950. Tour of Flanders 1942 and 1946. Paris-Tours 1946 and 1947. Paris-Brussels 1946 and 1952. Second in Tour de France 1948.

For a long time Schotte knew only one mode of transport—the bicycle.

Georges
Speicher
The King of Montlhéry

What struck us most about the man was his apparent detachment from the cycling scene. In this sense, Georges Speicher was even impressive. In 1933, for example, having won the Tour de France in late July, he made sure he had plenty of time of to celebrate. He went from reception to reception, somewhat losing his fine physical condition. The question: How, at that point, to have faith in him for the world championship, scheduled for mid-August at the Montlhéry autodrome just outside Paris? Quite logically, the selectors left him out of the French team. For Speicher the good life continued. There he was, the Friday before Sunday's world's, invited to a cinema on the Boulevard Ménilmontant to attend the premiere of a documentary film on his victorious Tour de France. He arrived by taxi. That evening one of the French team, Paul Chocque, pulled out of the race because of illness. As a result, the president of the French federation's athletic commission, Monsieur Legros, set off in search of Speicher, the team's first alternate. Learning that the rider had just left for the cinema, the federal official made haste. As Speicher stepped out of the taxi he was met by Legros, who greeted him with these words: "No cinema this evening, my dear Speicher; you are racing in the world championship on Sunday. Go home to bed!" It would take more than that to faze the winner of the Tour. The official had barely turned on his heel when the champion dove into the movie theater.

On the Sunday, Speicher was on the start line. The race unfolded under a heavy sky, though the threatening rain never fell. On every lap, as he passed the pits, Speicher had just one worry in his head: He had told some friends in the stands to remember to close the roof of his fine new car if it started raining. As the race unfolded, he became more and more interested in the battle for the rainbow jersey, and in the end he became the world champion. Second place, five minutes back, went to his teammate Antonin Magne, who had prepared for this race with great care, fine-tuning his strategy for several weeks. Speicher's victory made history: He was the first Frenchman—and one who had almost not competed—to became the world professional road champion.

He earned other laurels that season. *Miroir des Sports* magazine described him as follows: "What stands out most is his surprising ease, an ease that he has always possessed and which makes him, at twenty-six years of age, more like a young roadman with all his resources intact. Speicher wins 'easily,' just as he pedals 'easily,' adapts 'easily,' and recuperates 'easily.' This ease, to tell the truth, is something of a miracle. It is certain that in Speicher, we must above all admire a magnificent beast, a superb greyhound—slim, supple, purebred—a marvelous model of a road

racer, with long muscles, a deep lung capacity, and a resilient heart." Speicher was an average climber, but he proved to be a virtuoso in the descent. His elegant silhouette gave him the look of a wading bird. He was an unconditional supporter of the derailleur, a product still under debate for reasons of economy by most bike manufacturers. Since the derailleur had still not been authorized at the 1933 Tour, he devised a special assembly for the stirrup of the rear brake in an attempt to create a more sensible and progressive braking system. Beneath his apparent amateurism, Speicher was an observant and realistic technician. But above all, he became the king of Montlhéry, picking up three French titles on this circuit … and a certain world championship.

The general adoption of the derailleur owed much to Georges Speicher, the king of Montlhéry, here being congratulated by French music hall star Joséphine Baker.

GEORGES SPEICHER

Born: June 8, 1907, in Paris, France
Died: January 24, 1978
Palmarès: World Championship 1933. Tour de France 1933. Paris-Roubaix 1936. Paris-Arras 1931. Paris-Reims 1935. Paris-Angers 1935. Championship of France 1935, 1937, and 1939.

Philippe
Thys
The Basset Hound

This little Belgian, of average height but with a compact build, sat low in the saddle—hence his nickname, "the Basset Hound." Born in Anderlecht, Belgium, in 1890, he excelled in long-distance races and seemed ideally suited to the Tour de France. His palmarès certainly attests to this because he was the first in history to win the *Grande Boucle* three times—1913, 1914, and 1920. His record would surely have been infinitely richer without the interruption of World War I.

Philippe Thys first gained attention in the cycling world at the age of nineteen, when he put in a strong performance in the 1910 edition of the independent-category riders' Route de France, organized by Cycles Peugeot. His talent was confirmed the following year, when he dominated the race. Right away Léopold Alibert, the Peugeot professional team's *directeur sportif*, impressed with the young Belgian's class and drive, signed him on. He would be amply rewarded.

In his first pro season Thys finished the Tour de France in sixth place, and, in 1913 he won the first of his three Tour victories, a record that would not be matched until twenty-five years later, by Louison Bobet.

Thys accomplished much of his career in France, wearing the colors of the Vélo-club de Levallois. Besides the Tour, he won races such as the Belgian Championship, Paris-Tours, Paris-Toulouse, the Critérium des As, Paris-Lyon, and the Six Days of Brussels. He was a model of consistency. Normally calm, he became violently angry if someone dared to play a trick on him or took advantage of his trust. Take for example this anecdote from the 1920 Tour de France. At Mulhouse, during the Gex-Strasbourg stage, his compatriot Firmin Lambot remarked to him, "The roads are flat for the rest of the way. Why are you still in the small gear?" (This was in the days before derailleurs, when riders could choose between two gears, big and small, by turning the rear wheel around to

Thys was the first rider to win the Tour de France three times.

put the chain on a different cog.) Thys descended from his machine and began to reverse his wheel. At that moment Lambot, taking advantage of his deceit, took off. Thys caught him only after some solid turns of the pedal, and to prove to Lambot that such tricks were inappropriate, he beat him in the final sprint.

Not at all seduced by spectacular rides that thrilled the crowds, Thys was one of those riders who could stubbornly follow any pace and knew how to wait patiently until an opponent made a mistake. He had a certain serenity of effort, the serenity of an exceptional, self-assured man. All his movements were controlled; there was never an abrupt motion, rarely a turn of the pedal more uneven than the next. He weighed exactly the same—69 kilos (152 pounds)—at the finish of the Tour as at the start. This dependable regularity made him a champion of endurance, the ideal Tour de France rider. He won his third Tour at the age of thirty, seven years after his first win. Of the classics, he picked up Paris-Tours and the Tour of Lombardy in 1917. The war was still raging then, but Thys, aided by his prestige and appointed as a sergeant in the air force, took advantage of his status to stay in top shape.

Retiring from racing at age thirty-seven, he developed a passion for another sport—archery—and became the highly respected president of the Bienfaiteurs, an archery society in Brussels.

Throughout his career Philippe Thys had the habit of getting up in the middle of the night and going out on the roads, then watching the sun come up. He did not indulge himself. For this reason, his career was one of enlightening and comforting morality.

PHILIPPE THYS

Born: October 8, 1890, in Anderlecht, Belgium
Died: January 16, 1971
Palmarès: Tour de France 1913, 1914, and 1920. Paris-Tours 1917. Tours-Paris 1918. Tour of Lombardy 1917. Paris-Dijon-Paris 1921, 1922, and 1923. Critérium des As 1921.

René
Vietto
Bellhop and King

At the 1934 Tour de France an unknown little racer from Cannes—a former bell-hop at the Palm Beach Casino named René Vietto—suddenly took off in the moun-tains, winning three stages in five days. He had trained for the Tour on the roads of the Alps and easily conquered the steepest passes. From mountain to mountain, the renown of the young champion—with skin and hair of

brown, intentionally taciturn—continued to grow. His fame reached an all-time high one day in the Pyrenees when he stopped and gave up his bike to Antonin Magne, his team leader and *maillot jaune*, who had wrecked his front wheel in a crash. His infinitely grand gesture made all of France teary-eyed. The image of the young kid sacrificing his own chances of winning the Tour de France made Vietto's popularity surge. But let's return to the lofty feats that made Vietto the idol of a country brimming over with noble and generous sentiments. He was only twenty years old at the start of his first Tour de France in 1934. Compared with his French teammates, such as former Tour winner Magne, Georges Speicher, and the gifted Robert Lapébie, he did not carry much weight. He performed brilliantly in the mountains, but that was not a huge sur-prise. Wasn't he chosen for the national team on account of his climbing ability? Vietto had just won the Grand Prix Wolber, and many believed that the time had come for him to rub shoulders with the "giants."

A week into the race he won the two great alpine stages: Aix-les-Bains to Grenoble, via the Galibier, and Gap to Digne, over the Vars and Allos Passes. Already certain columnists were quick to remark that "the kid" was proving to be the purest high-mountain climber French cycling had ever known.

Unfortunately, Vietto would never win the *Grande Boucle*. The closest he would come was in 1939. After taking the lead on the fourth day at Lorient, he wore the *maillot jaune* for eleven days. Ironically, it was on his chosen terrain—the high mountains—that he lost the lead to the Belgian Sylvère Maës. Vietto—who finished the Tour in second place—was no longer the winged climber. And then World War II broke out.

When he was a bellhop at the Palm Beach Casino in Cannes, René Vietto dreamed of life in yellow. And so it was, in the 1947 Tour de France.

In 1947, when the Tour resumed, Vietto was still the darling of the French public. So many years of suffering had not made the fans forget. The sports-minded citizens of France were hoping for his victory. Vietto, pressured to prove that he had lost nothing of his abilities, attacked early on in the second stage as the race went through Valenciennes. At first accompanied by several others, the French climber, though far from his favorite terrain, decided to get the better of the Belgians and pushed on alone. There were cries of the "suicide of the French team" and of "Vietto's folly." It seemed like a crazy move. Still 80 kilometers from the finish in Brussels, he continued with his long solo effort. Stage victory and the *maillot jaune* were his, but how much had he taken out of himself?

Vietto was still in the race lead three days from the finish. Then came a marathon time-trial stage of 139 kilometers, traversing Brittany from coast to coast, from Vannes to Saint-Brieuc. It was a challenge that he wasn't up to.

"We no longer understood René," wrote Abel Michéa in the French daily *L'Humanité*. "He alone understood. And on the road, alone with his suffering, he had dignity. He had isolated himself in his defeat. He was ped-aling as if he were in another world…. And René cried about this Tour de France that he would never win. There was one moment when we rediscovered our René—when he flung his bike in the face of a team-mate who was attempting to give him a lesson in strategy: 'What strategy! It was two strong legs that I needed today!'"

René dragged his old legs around races for several more years, with his philosophy serene and his words incisive—but there was always, in the pocket of the *maillot jaune*, next to the heart, the regret of that 139-kilometer time-trial stage "that they put there just for me."

RENÉ VIETTO

Born: February 17, 1914, in Rocheville–Le Cannet, France
Died: October 14, 1988
Palmarès: Grand Prix Wolber 1934. Paris-Nice 1935. Circuit du Midi 1943. Grand Prix de la République 1946. Best climber of the Tour de France 1934.

ARISTOCRATS OF THE SPRINT

Just as speed is the aristocracy of movement, so it makes sense in our eyes to present the sprinters as the aristocrats of the cycling peloton—although their methods of dealing with problems, how they live, and the tactics they use to win usually do not reflect the best manners. By their very essence, sprinters have a "brutal" style, both toward themselves and even more so toward their opponents.

Sprint finishes vary infinitely. The swiftest riders use what the Italians call *scatto,* a last-minute punch to the line, to get clear of a rival or key off a lead-out rider who has prepared the final approach.

The following portraits have been sketched according to parameters that do not essentially favor the pure, tough sprinters such as Germany's Erik Zabel, six-time winner of the points classification at the Tour de France, but instead single out those—such as Darrigade, Maertens, Saronni, and Van Looy—who, by the totality of their performance, were seen as "complete" road racers. In short, aristocrats....

Rudi
Altig
Of Germany

Before the rise of Jan Ullrich and Erik Zabel, the best cyclist to come out of Germany was undoubtedly Rudi Altig from Mannheim. A veritable force of nature, with Herculean shoulders and a weight lifter's torso, Altig first gained notice as an amateur racer in 1959. On the Olympic track in Amsterdam, he won the world 4,000-meter pursuit championship, and later in the year he broke world amateur records for indoor tracks at the 1-kilometer and 5,000-meter distances.

In the individual pursuit race, his times were better than those of most professionals. This big blond kid merged power and flexibility, speed and endurance, and had a curious combination of ambition and lightheartedness.

When he had nothing more to learn in the amateur ranks, Altig decided to move up to the next level and, in order to improve, he moved to France. He remained a pursuiter long enough to become a two-time world champion at the pro level. But soon he focused on road racing, and his career truly took off in 1962 after he joined the St. Raphaël-Gitane team of Jacques Anquetil. It started with a sort of lèse-majesté crime: During the Vuelta a España, Altig not only claimed for himself the luxury of winning six stages and the points

At the famed Nürburgring in 1966, cheered on by his fellow Germans, Altig (right) defeated Anquetil and Poulidor to win his finest title: world road champion.

classification but also forced his team leader to let him take the overall victory. Anquetil quickly forgot the brashness of his new lieutenant, however, when a couple of months later Altig won the opening stage of his first Tour de France. The German even went on to take two more stages—and the green jersey.

In a crowning end to the season, Anquetil and Altig found themselves at the Baracchi Trophy, a challenging 111-kilometer, two-man team time trial in Italy. The Frenchman's fluid style did not fit well with the destructive, high-powered pulls of the German. After a fall, Anquetil finished the event in agony, dragged along for the last 50 kilometers by a lieutenant proud of his strength.

Altig's fighter's physique prevented him from excelling in the high mountains; he usually had to be content with partial successes in the great stage races. On the other hand, he shone a thousand times brighter in the one-day races—winning the Tour of Flanders, Milan–San Remo, and the world championship. He won his world title in 1966 in his own country, on the rugged Nürburgring, where he narrowly defeated Anquetil, with Raymond Poulidor in third place.

In this rainbow race things had started out badly for the racer from Mannheim. Sick and vomiting, convinced that he had no chance, he

slowly worked his way forward. On the final lap of the unusually long circuit, he successively passed Gianni Motta of Italy, Jean Stablinski of France, Eddy Merckx of Belgium, and others before catching Anquetil and Poulidor. Could he have hoped for better—especially as the year before, at the world's in San Sebastian, he was also in the finale just after recovering from a severe fracture of the femur?

Altig, once again wearing a world championship jersey, became a true hero in Germany, where the federal authorities awarded him the Silber Lorbeer, his country's highest honor.

RUDI ALTIG

Born: March 18, 1937, in Mannheim, Germany
Palmarès: World Championship 1966. Vuelta a España 1962. Tour of Flanders 1964. Milan–San Remo 1968. Grand Prix of Frankfurt 1970. Baracchi Trophy 1962 (with Jacques Anquetil). Green jersey of Tour de France 1962.

André Darrigade
The Greyhound of the Landes

With his ruddy complexion, blond locks, and talkative nature, this native of Dax in southwest France was one of his country's most noted sprinters. André Darrigade had the all-or-nothing approach to cycling, never afraid to "put his nose in the wind," as the French like to say. He had the liberality and the taste for panache of a true master. So much did he throw his heart into the job to make use of his famous finishing speed that he never let down his hardworking teammates. Though this moral high ground cost him dearly, it also brought him great success, crowned by a world championship.

Darrigade, who often raced with Louison Bobet and Jacques Anquetil on the French national team at the Tour de France, always put their needs ahead of his own. Even when it was his turn to shoot for a stage win, he first made sure to carry out his team duties—without a complaint. Depending on the circumstances, he would be free to pursue his own chances only on the approach to the finish, and often he'd be asked to sacrifice his personal ambition to help his team leaders—especially if they were in difficulties. An exceptional roadman-sprinter, Darrigade wore the Tour yellow jersey nineteen times; twice won the green jersey, in 1959 and 1961; and became the world road champion in 1959 at Zandvoort, on the shores of the North Sea. He dreamed of winning that world championship after placing third in the previous two years; it was the victory that he

longed for. Even so, he had many doubts prior to the 1959 championship race. On arriving in the Netherlands several days before the event, he was overcome by a raging toothache and then discovered the day before the start that he was carrying a tapeworm. This problem hadn't prevented him from riding a good Tour de France. And so?

Barely a quarter of the way into the 292-kilometer race a dozen riders went clear, Darrigade among them. The breakaway would stay away to the end, but the victory was by no means a foregone conclusion for the rapid Frenchman.

"We entered the last straightaway," Darrigade recounted, "Geldermans [of the Netherlands] in the lead and me right behind him, and I made sure that Foré [of Belgium] and Simpson [of Britain] stayed behind me. I then let Gismondi [of Italy] wear himself out at the front for a few moments before I made my move about a hundred meters before the line. Gismondi soon sat up, so fifty meters before the finish banner, I had the race won. World champion … you're going to be the world champion … you are the world champion! Those thoughts swirled in my head for a few unforgettable seconds. It was the thrill of a lifetime, something I'd never experience again."

His specialty: winning the first stage at the Tour de France (below, in 1958). His strength: a fierce desire to finish at all costs, as in the finale of this 1955 Paris-Brussels (left page).

ANDRÉ DARRIGADE

Born: April 24, 1929, in Narrosse, near Dax (Landes), France
Palmarès: World Championship 1959. French Championship 1955. Tour of Lombardy 1956. Critérium National 1959. Baracchi Trophy 1956 (with Rolf Graf). Twenty-two stages of the Tour de France. Green jersey of Tour de France 1959 and 1961.

Fred
Debruyne
The Flahute

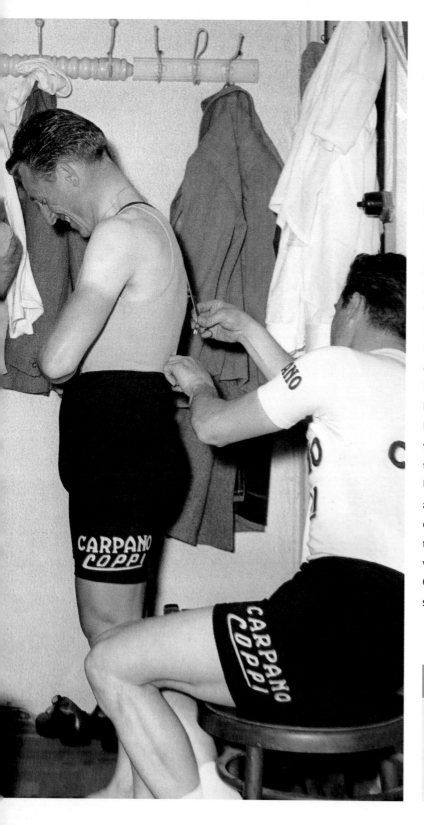

Fred Debruyne had a remarkable tactical mind, a great turn of speed, and all the other attributes of a winner. His all-around qualities enabled him to win for three consecutive years (1956–1958) the Challenge Desgrange-Colombo, then the unofficial, season-long world championship, based on results in the major classics and stage races. Debruyne, born in the heart of Flanders, had his biggest successes in the classics. Other than two victories at Paris-Nice, which confirmed his talents as a stage racer, the Flahute won Milan–San Remo, the Tour of Flanders, Paris-Roubaix, Liège-Bastogne-Liège (three times), and Paris-Tours.

A devoted teammate and a strong leader, this charming racer won the early praise of Antonin Magne, then the respected *directeur sportif* of the Mercier team, but Debruyne wasn't favored by circumstances. In a sense he came to pro racing too early because he was overshadowed by his illustrious countryman Rik Van Steenbergen. He also came too late because Rik Van Looy's budding glory left him no slack.

"Caught between two opposing Vans," wrote French racer-turned-broadcaster Jean Bobet, "Fred appears a bit like the gentleman distressed to find himself caught in a draft of air." But on the bike the drafts did not bother him. He was clever, and he knew how to conserve his strength and look after himself, sensing how the race was going rather than commanding it. His talents as a sprinter helped him take six stage wins at the Tour de France: three in 1954 and three in 1956. In truth, he excelled everywhere, though the high mountains were somewhat of a challenge for him. But he had no real interest in becoming a climber, as he knew he would never be an overall challenger in the grand tours. He preferred to invest his energy elsewhere. Debruyne's career came to an end in 1961, following a serious automobile accident the previous year, when he was driving with his fellow Belgian racer Willy Vannitsen. Debruyne managed the transition well. He was at first a Flemish-language reporter on cycling for Belgian television, then had spells as a *directeur sportif* and a press officer for pro racing teams. Using his skills as an intelligent and dynamic athlete, he gave a new image and a modern style to the somewhat old-fashioned identity of Flemish cycling. Along with his elegance and ability to speak many languages, this true gentleman brought a sense of professionalism to his sport. Having worn the purple jersey of the Mercier team and the white jersey of Carpano-Coppi, he also contributed significantly to the conversion of his sport into a viable multinational product.

A fervent sprinter and later an expert commentator,
Debruyne brought much to the sport.

FRED DEBRUYNE

Born: October 21, 1930, in Berlaere-les-Termonde, Belgium
Died: February 5, 1994
Palmarès: Milan–San Remo 1956. Liège-Bastogne-Liège 1956, 1958, and 1959. Tour of Flanders 1957. Paris-Roubaix 1957. Paris-Tours 1957. Paris-Nice 1956 and 1958.

Sean
Kelly
Fighting Spirit

He came from green Ireland, the third of four Kelly brothers. The one who would become the most famous. In his hometown of Carrick-on-Suir, a square was named after Sean Kelly, dedicated before a crowd of six thousand townsfolk in 1982 after his victory in the points classification of the Tour de France. He would win the famous green jersey three times.

The Kelly boys all worked on the family farm. Only Sean chose a different path. He joined the local cycling club in his midteens, and within three years he acquired an impressive number of victories. But nothing more may have happened had it not been for a correspondent of a Metz cycling club stationed in England who sent back to France regular reports of the young Irishman's successes—including a stage win at the then prestigious Milk Race Tour of Britain.

So Kelly left home to live in Metz, in the Lorraine region of northeast France, where he impressed the locals with his hard training and his many racing qualities that brought him dozens of victories. Young amateurs from Besançon, in awe of Kelly's finishing speed, recommended the Irishman to Jean de Gribaldy, a pro team *directeur sportif* and well-known talent scout. De Gribaldy learned, however, that the young sprinter had taken off— Kelly was homesick and had returned to Tipperary. Not to be deterred, the Besançon aristocrat phoned Sean at the Kelly farm to offer him a pro contract. The Irishman believed he was too young to enter the jungle of professional cycling, but de Gribaldy was relentless. He flew his private plane to Dublin, then took a taxi to Carrick. The Frenchman's persuasive language bore fruit, and Sean eventually surrendered and signed on the dotted line.

In January 1977 Kelly left for Besançon to join de Gribaldy's French branch of the Belgian squad, Flandria, racing alongside the Belgian stars Freddy Maertens, Marc Demeyer, and Michel Pollentier. Kelly won a stage of the Tour de France in his second season with Flandria, but, feeling uncomfortable and too dependent on Maertens within the team, Sean left Jean de Gribaldy. He

moved to Vilvoorde in Belgium and had three years with the Splendor team, continuing to pick up stage wins at the Tour and Vuelta a España. But Kelly's career didn't really take off until 1982, when he returned to de Gribaldy to lead the Sem France team.

De Gribaldy's great advantage was the understanding that Kelly had at his disposal all the attributes of an all-around racer—power, speed, an excellent vision of the race, and an unflagging fighting spirit. The French

director also knew that Kelly had to see himself as a winner, so he allowed the Irishman complete freedom to lead the team.

Kelly's breakthrough came that first spring with Sem France when he won the overall victory at the then ten-day Paris–Nice—a race he would win seven years in succession. His other breakthrough came in October 1983, when Kelly narrowly outsprinted world champion Greg LeMond and Dutchman Adri Van der Poel to win the Tour of Lombardy—his first victory in a major classic.

Kelly certainly continued to experience some psychological blocks, but his already great experience helped him to acquire ten wins in the big classics such as Paris-Roubaix, along with his successes in stage racing. Besides winning Paris-Nice seven times, the Irishman took the Tour of Switzerland twice, and the Vuelta. In contrast, the Tour de France created problems for him—he rarely performed well at the highest altitudes, especially if there were a number of mountain stages in a row, and his best overall result was fourth in 1984.

Kelly was a simple man. He was at his happiest when the month of November arrived and he could return to Ireland with his wife, Linda, and settle in with his brother-in-law in a quiet country house. For several weeks, cycling would be just a memory. Kelly kept in shape with daily runs in the Carrick hills, weight training, massage, and a sauna twice a week. He was a great professional. By staying active throughout the winter, he remained faithful to one of the principles of Jean de Gribaldy: "He who takes good care of himself in the winter will win races in the summer."

Sean Kelly like a wild animal tearing toward the finish of Milan–San Remo in 1992 (left page), and outsprinting Greg LeMond to win the 1983 Tour of Lombardy (above), his first classic victory.

SEAN KELLY

Born: May 21, 1956, in Carrick-on-Suir, Ireland
Palmarès: Paris-Roubaix 1984 and 1986. Tour of Lombardy 1983, 1985, and 1991. Milan–San Remo 1986 and 1992. Liège-Bastogne-Liège 1984 and 1989. Blois-Chaville (Paris-Tours) 1984. Vuelta a España 1986. Paris-Nice 1982, 1983, 1984, 1985, 1986, 1987, and 1988. Tour of Switzerland 1983 and 1990. Grand Prix des Nations 1986. Critérium International 1983, 1984, and 1987. Green jersey of Tour de France 1982, 1983, and 1985.

Freddy **Maertens**
Glory and Despair

Freddy Maertens, a superb natural athlete from Nieuwport on Belgium's North Sea coast, developed his cycling skills at a young age. When he was twelve he rode his bike two hours before school every morning to deliver newspapers. As an adolescent he followed a harsh training regimen, often in the fierce winds blowing off the ocean. By age nineteen, in 1971, he was the amateur champion of Belgium and placed second in the world championship. From that point on, it was clear that this unusual kid, endowed with the qualities of a champion, was destined for a great cycling career.

When he turned pro, he had to fight hard against the Belgian establishment at the time of Eddy Merckx, Roger De Vlaeminck, and Frans Verbeeck. But Maertens had true class, and he soon made a name for himself. However, though his triumphs leave little room for doubt, Freddy certainly experienced some dark times along the way. His athletic career was like an odyssey. At age twenty-one, he came dramatically close to winning the world championship in Barcelona, just losing to Felice Gimondi after having followed orders to lead out the sprint for Merckx, the Belgian team leader. After that near miss everyone knew he would eventually take the world title. Freddy's day came in 1976, at Ostuni, Italy, where he readily beat Italian superstar Francesco Moser. By taking the world championship, he had reached the top of his profession. Maertens shone on all terrain—time trials, classics, and stage races. Certainly he wasn't great in the high mountains, but nevertheless, he won the Vuelta a España in 1977 and walked away with no fewer than twelve stage wins.

The Belgians were convinced that they had a new Merckx in their midst. But Maertens's momentum clearly broke at the Giro d'Italia in 1977 at the end of the eighth stage, on the racetrack at Mugello. A spectacular fall after a collision with Rik Van Linden in the mass finishing sprint left Maertens with a fractured wrist and kept him off the bike for a long time. Gossip linked his name to doping, and it was whispered that his healing was slowed by forbidden substances administered to him to increase his muscular strength. Financial complications and judicial entanglements also devastated Maertens. He thought he would never emerge from the abyss. Then a miracle happened. The Belgian returned unexpectedly and dramatically to the forefront of the scene at the 1981 Tour de France. Regaining all his great sprinting abilities, he won five stages and the points classification. There he was, selected for the Belgian team at the world championships in Prague.

Five years after having captured the rainbow jersey in a southern Italian town, he regained the supreme title in the capital of Czechoslovakia. He who several months before had no longer been a force in the peloton delivered one of the most extraordinary comebacks of all time. In Prague about thirty men were at the head of the race as they prepared for the final rush. Giuseppe Saronni, with several Italian teammates to help him, was poised to win the sprint, but his teammate Gibi Baronchelli started the lead-out too soon for Saronni, and Maertens passed him several meters before the finish.

Curiously, this was the last great victory for Freddy Maertens. He then wore himself out in the criteriums, trying to put away a bit of money. The following year the rainbow jersey was no longer seen at the head of the peloton. He finished few races, still obtained a few contracts, and changed teams each year. He clung in vain to the sport that had given him everything— glory, wealth, and, finally, despair.

Contrary to appearances, life was not all roses for Freddy Maertens.

FREDDY MAERTENS

Born: February 13, 1952, in Nieuwport, Belgium
Palmarès: World Championship 1976 and 1981. Vuelta a España 1977. Tour of Belgium 1975. Paris-Nice 1977. Paris-Brussels 1975. Tours-Versailles (Paris-Tours) 1975. Grand Prix des Nations 1976. Baracchi Trophy 1976 (with Michel Pollentier). Amstel Gold Race 1976. Flèche Wallonne 1977. Green jersey of Tour de France 1976, 1978, and 1981.

Fiorenzo **Magni**
The Lion of Flanders

It was in Belgium, in Flanders, that this balding Italian earned much of his fame. Practically isolated in a pack of formidable Flemish road racers, Fiorenzo Magni met the challenge superbly, under difficult conditions, in three consecutive years—marking a unique triple in the annals of the Tour of Flanders.

On these narrow and sometimes cobblestone-paved roads, Magni imposed his relentless authority—that of a strong, magnificent athlete, well prepared and completely resistant to bitter weather, particularly snow or rain. While many of his opponents raided cafés and restaurants to warm themselves, he fought through the pain to forge the three victories that earned him the nickname "the Lion of Flanders." In 1949 he won in a sprint, while in 1950 and 1951 he attacked on the infamous Mur de Grammont. Although Magni had a definite talent for one-day racing, he also distinguished himself in stage racing, thanks to his invincible temperament. His great courage helped him win the Giro d'Italia three times. For Magni everything seemed to come in threes as he also won three Italian Championships, three Baracchi Trophies, and three Tours of Piedmont. At the Tour de France he won seven stages, including the final one at the

Parc des Princes in 1953. Despite those satisfactions, the Tour left Magni with his greatest regret. In 1950 he was wearing the *maillot jaune* when Gino Bartali, complaining that he had been roughed up by spectators when he had fallen on the Col d'Aspin, ordered the two Italian teams—both the national squad and the young riders team—to withdraw from the Tour. So Magni had to pack up his treasured yellow jersey and return to Italy. Magni was just as much a pioneer in developing the sport off the bike. In 1954, when the bicycle manufacturers that sponsored all the pro cycling teams experienced a severe development crisis, threatening the very life of the sport, he made a deal to save his team. The deal was with Nivea, a maker of beauty creams, which became the title sponsor. Magni's blue jersey bore the inscription "Nivea-Fuchs," and the first noncycling team sponsor was born. It was the start of cycling's big commercial revolution.

Handicapped by a fractured clavicle, Magni gripped a handlebar-tape "rope" with his teeth to help pull him up the climbs in Lombardy in 1954.

FIORENZO MAGNI

Born: December 7, 1920, in Vaiano di Prato
Palmarès: Giro d'Italia 1948, 1951, 1955. Tour of Flanders 1949, 1950, and 1951. Rome-Naples-Rome 1952 and 1953. Tour of Piedmont 1953 and 1956. Tour of Tuscany 1949 and 1954. Baracchi Trophy 1949 (with Adolfo Grosso), 1950 (with Antonio Bevilacqua), and 1951 (with Giuseppe Minardi). Italian Championship 1951, 1953, and 1954.

Constant
Ockers
The Crafty One

He was small (five feet five inches) and slender (134 pounds), but what energy was contained in that little frame! For many years, Constant "Stan" Ockers was seen as a terrible "wheel-sucker," but he made himself the master of this type of exercise: Nobody could drop him. One day he became bolder, seized control, and won some impressive victories. Ockers became the world champion on a scorching August day in 1955 on the Frascati circuit in the outskirts of Rome—a victory he owed to no one but himself. Halfway through the 293-kilometer race, a lead group containing André Darrigade, Antonin Rolland, Jacques Anquetil, Pasquale Fornara, Gastone Nencini, and Miguel Poblet was more than three minutes ahead of Raphaël Geminiani and Jean-Pierre Schmitz. Within the peloton, more than five minutes back, Fausto Coppi and defending champion Louison Bobet faced each other like dueling brothers, neither wanting to help the other organize a chase. The pack had fallen still farther behind when, one by one, riders began to sneak away—first Marcel Janssens, then Bruno Monti, Pierre Molinéris and … Ockers. Stan dropped Monti and Molinéris in the twelfth of the fourteen laps, caught the leaders during the next-to-last lap, and attacked almost immediately on the course's main climb. No one could follow him, and, as night began to fall on the hills of Rome, the little Belgian placed the rainbow jersey on his shoulders.

Thirteen and a half months later, on September 29, 1956, Ockers suffered a tragic fall at Antwerp's indoor velodrome, just a few steps from home. He was unable to avoid a spectator hanging too far over the edge of the wooden track, and in a breathtaking somersault, the Belgian racer crashed and fractured his skull. Two days later he died without having regained consciousness.

An athlete with great stamina, excellent at racing on all types of terrain, Ockers was first discovered by the French in the 1946 Monaco-Paris, the five-day race that "replaced" the Tour de France prior to its postwar return. Unfortunately, though he was looking like a true winner, he was forced to drop out when a dog threw itself beneath his wheels and caused him to crash. Afterward, in the real Tour de France, he was always a strong contender, with two second-place finishes: in 1950, behind Ferdi Kubler, and in 1952, behind Fausto Coppi. He shone equally brightly on the roads of the Ardennes, pulling off the double victory in the Flèche Wallonne and Liège-Bastogne-Liège in 1955—his greatest year.

They called him "the stingy rider," but he was simply efficient in his efforts; "the lazy one," but he was in fact very clever; and "the crafty one," but he was actually a great strategist.

Stan Ockers had grown up in the port town of Antwerp, on the docks. Grease and oil colored his childhood, and his ears were accustomed to the background music of ships' sirens. Naturally enough, his first steps led him toward the sea, with thoughts of travel. Too young to enlist in the Royal Belgian Navy, he became a painter, working on the docks and ships' hulls. He was too shy to ask permission to board. His working hours were tied to those of the port, and Stan watched with envy as neighborhood friends went out on their bikes on Sundays. He confided this childish sorrow to his older brother, who, first amused, then interested, agreed to give the boy his first bicycle. Within a few years Stan passed every test offered by amateur racing and turned pro. His debut at the Tour of Switzerland was stunning—he placed second behind Coppi in the time-trial stage at an average speed of 46 kilometers per hour. All bets were open on the young man from Antwerp.

Winning the Flèche Wallonne in 1953, Ockers finally entered the league of the greats (left). Two years later he became the world champion (right page).

CONSTANT "STAN" OCKERS

Born: February 3, 1920 in Borgerhout, Belgium
Died: October 1, 1956
Palmarès: World Championship 1955. Flèche Wallonne 1953 and 1955. Liège-Bastogne-Liège 1955. Tour of Belgium 1948. Rome-Naples-Rome 1956. Green jersey of Tour de France 1955 and 1956. Second in Tour de France 1950 and 1952.

Giuseppe
Saronni
Il Beppe

Less than two years after he entered the pro circuit, Giuseppe Saronni was already one of the sport's leading stars. Not only was he the youngest-ever Italian professional (at age nineteen), but he also would become the Giro d'Italia's youngest winner (at twenty-one). His ascendancy was not long in coming, but he had to work hard to adjust to the tough world of professional racing after breezing through his amateur career, in which he acquired an amazing 127 victory bouquets.

His parents were from Lombardy, but he grew up in Novara, in the heart of Piedmont. In his family everyone raced bikes. His father, Romano, had excelled as an amateur on the Italian tracks, competing against great sprinters such as Sante Gaiardoni. Unfortunately, an accident forced him to end his racing career. Giuseppe's oldest brother, Antonio, also became a professional and specialized in cyclo-cross. The third child of the family, Alberto, became an excellent junior racer, and Patricia, the only daughter, was also plagued by the demon of cycling.

But only Giuseppe, nicknamed "Beppe," would reach the highest level in his sport, at a time when the *tifosi* had eyes for no one but Francesco Moser, who won the world championship in 1977, the year Saronni turned pro. Saronni was a controversial figure. At first he was reproached for progressing too slowly, and even for not progressing at all. From 1977 to 1980 he wasn't exactly unsuccessful, but in the major races he was in a rut, with a series of second-place finishes—three at Milan–San Remo, two more at the Flèche Wallonne, and another at Blois-Chaville (the 1970s version of Paris-Tours). Finally he won the Giro and started a rivalry that feverishly divided the peninsula into Moser and Saronni fanatics, as in the most glorious days of Coppi and Bartali.

In 1981 Beppe wasn't yet twenty-four years old when he set his sights on the world road championship, which took place in Prague that year. He believed he had the victory in his grasp, but Freddy Maertens came

out of nowhere and handed Saronni another second place. True, by this time his palmarès included a Flèche Wallonne victory, but it was not enough. He believed that hard work would pay off, so he buckled down to developing his career—just as he had done as a teenaged apprentice in the Olivetti factories, repairing calculators and typewriters.

What was the true caliber of this young champion who so often came up short? He was intelligent and clever. What was he missing? Perhaps what he lacked was a capacity for suffering. He often gave the impression of being a blue blood incapable of withstanding physical pain—a thoroughbred racehorse that the jockey had to teach to be less fearful of its rivals' behavior.

But the Italian matured. He prepared himself both mentally and physically for the 1982 world championship at Goodwood, England. His failure in Prague, the year before, was like a lump in his throat. He wanted to erase it as quickly as possible. And his wish was granted. Launching his uphill sprint with an extraordinary burst of energy, Saronni passed all his opponents with 300 meters still to go, to finish ahead of Greg LeMond and Sean Kelly. The Italian appeared liberated. Here was the breakthrough major victory he had been seeking. Others soon followed: the Tour of Lombardy, Milan–San Remo, and a second Giro.

At the same time his relations with Moser had normalized. Still fierce rivals at the races, they were no longer enemies in daily life. They agreed one day, without the least reluctance, to race the two-man Baracchi Trophy time trial together. What a beautiful sight! Who would have predicted this spectacular reconciliation? It was a magnificent image of a reunited Italy.

Beppe had his finest year after winning the rainbow jersey in 1982.

GIUSEPPE SARONNI

Born: September 22, 1957, in Novara, Italy
Palmarès: World Championship 1982. Giro d'Italia 1979 and 1983. Tour of Switzerland 1982. Tour de Romandie 1979. Tour of Lombardy 1982. Flèche Wallonne 1980. Milan–San Remo 1983. Championship of Zürich 1979. Baracchi Trophy 1979 (with Francesco Moser).

Rik
Van Looy
The Emperor of Herentals

Until Van Looy appeared on the scene, the cycling world had given the title of King of the Classics to Rik Van Steenbergen. But as soon as he had taken his place among the professionals, "Rik II," as he was nicknamed, ran riot in the one-day races. Over the years he won them all, though he had to wait until the age of thirty-five to take the last of his collection, the Flèche Wallonne.

Van Looy held an intermediary reign that served as a link between two other Belgian superstars, Van Steenbergen and Eddy Merckx. Less eclectic than the first, less complete than the second, he merged style with power, adding a certain refinement to his natural brute strength. He was neither boastful nor modest. He considered it a weakness to show kindness or generosity toward a defeated opponent, just as he judged it shameful to kowtow to a winner.

Rik Van Looy was undoubtedly the king of sprinters, and the victories won thanks to his finishing speed were innumerable. The Belgian had another rare quality: He was a natural attacker who had a "feel" for a race like no one else. He knew how to take advantage of his opponents and let them wear themselves out before the finish. He also knew how to build a formidable support team, which became known as the Red Guard, so called because of the color of his Solo team jerseys.

His greatest joy was sowing panic in the peloton with his remarkably powerful surges. He was unequaled in his ability to scatter the opposition on days when strong crosswinds were blowing. Conscious of his responsibilities as a team leader, he was a totally focused competitor and didn't let anything divert him from his supreme goal: victory.

Unlike the roadmen-sprinters of later years, Rik Van Looy always preferred to go on the offensive rather than play the waiting game. He usually forbade his teammates from starting breakaways, but he had no qualms about instigating them himself, even from a distance. He had a tremendous capacity for work and traveled to just about every event on the international calendar, from Sardinia to the Netherlands and from Spain to Italy, pausing in between in Belgium and France. He raced so much that one commentator pointed out that Van Looy rode his bike at least once around the world every year.

For him, the seasons blurred together. In winter he went with his team to the north of Italy for a training camp at Riva del Garda. Each day the training rides intensified. Van Looy was never one to leave anything to chance, and he embraced new technology. He was the first to use a curved fork in the spring classics, to help smooth out the long stretches of cobblestones in races such as Paris–Roubaix. And he was one of the pioneers of using silk tubular tires in road races, making sure they were properly "cured" by storing them in his workshop for up to eight years. Many called him a tyrant for insisting that he control everything within his team, and he could never stand to repeat an order. In his defense, though, he made sure that all of his teammates were paid very well.

Van Looy built a palmarès that matched his prestige—winning in particular three Paris–Roubaix and two world championships. He started the Tour de France seven times and won seven stages, but he only once wore the yellow jersey, in 1965, between Cologne and Liège. During his first Tour in 1962, at the age of twenty-eight, he was knocked over by a motorcyclist on the eleventh stage, Bayonne–Pau, and had to quit. The following year, though, his aggressive riding and rapid sprint earned him the green jersey as winner of the points classification.

Van Looy was one of the most spectacular champions in history, and in his seventeen years as a professional cyclist he won 379 victories.

With his natural, animal-like strength, Van Looy built a palmarès as thick as a phone book.

RIK VAN LOOY

Born: December 20, 1933, in Grobbendonk, Belgium
Palmarès: World Championship 1960 and 1961. Paris–Roubaix 1961, 1962, and 1965. Tour of Flanders 1959 and 1962. Liège–Bastogne–Liège 1961. Flèche Wallonne 1968. Paris–Tours 1959 and 1967. Tour of Lombardy 1959. Milan–San Remo 1958. Tour of Belgium 1961. Green jersey of Tour de France 1963.

Rik
Van Steenbergen
Stone Mountain

Rik Van Steenbergen ranks among the finest and most eclectic champions of his century. This athletic Belgian, born on the Dutch border, was as brilliant on the track as on the road. For more than twenty years, this "stone mountain" (as his name translates into English) established himself as the genuine Superman of cycling, moving from season to season, summer to winter, without a break. A stunning sprinter and an incomparable tactician, he possessed the strength of a prizefighter and the kind of class that earned the respect of all his opponents. He would almost certainly have been more successful on the road if he had agreed to a little more moderation in his schedule. The proof needed to confirm this assessment came at the 1951 Giro d'Italia, when he finished in second place, only 1:46 behind winner Fiorenzo Magni, by getting the most out of himself every day. In this three-week race he gave the most convincing demonstration of his potential, battling hard, even in the mountains. Van Steenbergen began his professional career in 1943 by winning three national championships—the road race, individual pursuit, and track omnium. He was not yet nineteen. His victories would continue unabated for twenty years. He won the Tour of Flanders in 1944 and again in 1946. In 1948 he took Paris-Roubaix, riding at a then record average speed of 43.6 kilometers per hour. The following year he added the Flèche Wallonne to his palmarès, then won the world road championship in Copenhagen, beating two other all-time greats, Ferdi Kubler and Fausto Coppi.

The massive Belgian's primary weapon was his incomparable sprinting power. That quality made him a wonderful track racer, particularly on

the winter's six-day circuit. Apart from his successes at the Giro, we shouldn't forget that he took part in three Tours de France, winning a total of four stages. In the 1952 edition he won at Rennes on the first day, capturing the *maillot jaune*. He also won the Tour de l'Ouest, then a major nine-day stage race.

Van Steenbergen impressed all the giants of the peloton, from Coppi to Hugo Koblet to Louison Bobet. Given his prestige, especially in Belgium, he should have conducted himself more like a gentleman. But he was withdrawn in every interaction and avoided most contact with the public. He appeared indifferent to those around him. In truth, he expressed himself completely only on a bike. Raphaël Geminiani, a fellow racer, said of Van Steenbergen: "He was the cold Fleming—reticent, with a cloud of problems creasing his brow—but he held his head high. He was most at ease with a pair of handlebars in his hands, ready to race, on demand, no matter the race or the competition. I have seen him contest the most minor lap prize, for this person who one day would become so extraordinary started out with the soul of a mercenary. He was a man of contrasts."

Addressing a group of young Belgian cyclists one day, Van Steenbergen declared, "Do you think my three world championship titles fell out of the sky like magic? Do you think I only had to show up for races to win them? Since my debut I have known just one law: my profession as a bike racer—a job that demands complete dedication."

Never did he start a race in mediocre condition; never did he fail to give value for his start money. His high work ethic and the persistence of his training regimen allowed him to race until he was forty-three years old. In 1957 he managed the feat of racing first in the Belgian Congo, then in Copenhagen forty-eight hours later, followed in the next couple of days by races in Paris and Rocourt. It was an extraordinary accomplishment in the days before jet-powered air travel: from Africa to Denmark to France to Belgium, and winning every race!

Van Steenbergen did not have much time for humor. To him, racing relationships were strictly professional in nature. "I remember," recounted another French racer, Jean Bobet, "that in the rounds of post-Tour criterium races, the scenario was always the same. Hardly out of his car and without taking the time to say hello, he wanted to find out the time of the race, the address of a restaurant, the correct gear ratio to use, and the date by which he would be paid by the organizer. As for the rest, jokes and small talk, Rik had no time to waste. Across his brow, three large wrinkles testified to his constant preoccupation."

In Copenhagen in 1949 Rik won his rainbow jersey (upper left page), defeating Ferdi Kubler and Fausto Coppi (above).

RIK VAN STEENBERGEN

Born: September 9, 1924, in Arendonk, Belgium

Palmarès: World Championship 1949, 1956, and 1957. Paris-Roubaix 1948 and 1952. Tour of Flanders 1944 and 1946. Flèche Wallonne 1949 and 1958. Paris-Brussels 1950. Milan–San Remo 1954.

THE HEROIC ONES

If "courage in rugby is the least of things," to quote an old French expression, then heroism in cycling is something that flows through the streets, across the cobblestones, and through the mountains. This heroism exists from the moment that competitors arrive in the peloton who possess such magnificent qualities as drive, decisiveness, and self-transcendence. The riders whose names illuminate this chapter have known tumultuous, emotional, or, worse yet, tragic destinies. For example, Tom Simpson lost his life on the broiling slopes of Mont Ventoux; Roger Rivière tumbled into a ravine in the Cévennes; and Luis Ocaña's magnificent yellow jersey was blackened when he crashed in an apocalyptic rainstorm on a Pyrenean descent. Luckily, heroism does sometimes cross paths with glory, and the public still believes in miracles. Take for example Jean Robic's last-day attack that brought him victory at the 1947 Tour de France. But when the miracle endures, so that our lasting memory is one of inevitable victories, then the admiration carries a name. In this case, it is the name of a woman—Jeannie Longo. We salute her and all of cycling's other heroic ones.

Lucien
Aimar
The Price of Clairvoyance

In 1966 the Frenchman Lucien Aimar won the Tour de France, which came as a complete shock to most people. However, this solidly built rider from Hyères on the Côte d'Azur had shown signs of his great ability when he was still an amateur—certainly when he won the Route de France stage race but most of all when he lost, by default, the two-week Tour de l'Avenir in 1964. Aimar was given a one-minute penalty after he punched the Belgian racer Joseph Spruyt, handing the victory to Felice Gimondi—the Italian who would go on to win the Tour de France the following year.

Born in 1940, the impulsive yet seemingly austere Aimar gained the confidence of the Bic team *directeur sportif* Raphaël Geminiani, who, after signing him up in 1965, went so far as to predict the victory of his protégé in the Tour de France during his first years as a pro. The journalists thought this

prophecy was simply another of Geminiani's pipe dreams, a view that seemed to be confirmed when in the 1965 Tour de France Aimar blew up on the scorching slopes of the Aubisque Pass. He was not alone, though—the Italian star Vittorio Adorni also dropped out that day in the Pyrenees.

In 1966, at the height of the Anquetil-Poulidor rivalry, Aimar had little faith in his own chances of victory at the Tour. He had yet to prove himself as a professional. Circumstance and his own merit, however, would decide otherwise. His team leader, Jacques Anquetil, had lost his passion for racing, but Anquetil's archrival Raymond Poulidor remained dangerous. In the seventeenth stage, Briançon to Turin, the peloton grew lethargic under the hot sun, and race leader Jan Janssen let down his guard for a moment. Poulidor attacked with four others, and Aimar wasn't sure what to do. Anquetil stepped in and paced Aimar up to the Poulidor group. That was when Aimar leaped ahead, expertly negotiating the winding descent of the little Coletta Pass and disappearing from view. Poulidor gave up, and Janssen looked desperately for his teammates, but by the time he was able to regroup and begin the chase it was already too late. By the stage finish in Turin, Aimar had gained two minutes on Janssen and Poulidor to take the *maillot jaune,* and Anquetil laughed through his teeth at the smart tactical plan played against his eternal rival.

In the 1966 Tour de France, riding here between
Raymond Poulidor (to his right) and Roger Pingeon (to his left),
Lucien Aimar lived life in yellow and entered cycling history.

Poulidor did not want to admit defeat, though. The next day he attacked during the eighteenth stage, Ivrea to Chamonix, on the steep Forclaz Pass. But Anquetil again offered his services to his young leader, and they managed to limit Poulidor's gain to less than a minute.

No longer in a position to win the Tour, Anquetil was still getting the satisfaction of victory by proxy. The next day, suffering from congestion, he took his final bow from the race. Anquetil never returned to the Tour, but before his departure he placed his Ford France team at Aimar's disposal. Aimar no longer feared anything—his clairvoyance; his opportunism and his quick, instinctive ability to adapt to any situation; and his discipline in controlling his own impulsive character made him a magnificent winner.

LUCIEN AIMAR

Born: April 28, 1941, in Hyères, France
Palmarès: Tour de France 1966. French Championship 1968. Genoa-Nice 1966. Four Days of Dunkirk 1967. Polymultipliée 1970.

Raphaël
Geminiani
The Big Rifle

He had loads of class and character, and most of all a terrific personality. With his racy language, Raphaël Geminiani is remembered as much for his colorful stories as for claiming a place among the legends of cycling. Always ready to give everything he had, on the road as in life, he was the French stage-race specialist par excellence. In fact, he was one of the rare racers to wear the leader jersey at the Tours of France, Italy, and Spain, and he was the only one to win the title of best climber in all three grand tours.

He was called "the Big Rifle"—a name coined by Louison Bobet during the 1955 Tour de France after a stage in which Geminiani had successfully shut down Charly Gaul on his opponent's favored mountain terrain. In all, he spent seventeen years as a pro bike racer and competed in twelve Tours de France, winning seven stages.

A gritty worker, he never looked down on even the most unrewarding tasks. He was always willing to try the craziest moves, which often proved successful. Never did his angry outbursts overshadow his feats on the bike.

He was undeniably a fighter, and this quality was most evident in the intensity of his facial expressions and in his boundless energy.

Certainly Geminiani remains one of the monuments of cycling. But we cannot say enough about his ability to foresee the evolution of his sport. He was a pioneer—indeed, the first to introduce a noncycling brand into the French peloton, linking his surname with the aperitif that bore the sanctified version of his first name. The rise of the Geminiani–St. Raphaël team was undoubtedly one of the smartest ideas to be embraced by the sport.

It all came about at the end of 1953. Road racing was at a turning point in its history. Would the bike companies, until then the only ones to benefit from the publicity created by racing, give up their place as team sponsors to noncycling companies that had access to significant marketing budgets? French bike manufacturers refused to add other brand names on their team jerseys even though they were having a hard time economically. Many were sliding toward bankruptcy, threatening to take the entire cycling infrastructure down with them.

Geminiani was well aware of the danger, particularly when Rochet, which should have raised his salary after he won the French championship, instead proposed a 30 percent reduction. This intolerable situation led him to reach an agreement with a small manufacturer that agreed to build Geminiani bikes and help him form a new team. He knew how to be patient, for he believed that he was in the right, especially when the 1954 season continued to push the bike manufacturers toward ruin.

Because his first name was also a brand of aperitif, Geminiani designed an astute publicity plan. He paid a visit to the St. Raphaël–Quinquina company, which already invested much of its advertising budget in sports, and the advertising director quickly saw the promotional benefits of professional bike racers wearing jerseys bearing the name of his brand.

The French Cycling Federation wasn't keen to relinquish team sponsorship to noncycling companies. But in charge of the federation was Achille Joinard, who was also the acting president of the Union Cycliste Internationale (UCI), the sport's governing body. He was a reasonable man, and he knew which way the world was turning. He cracked open a door for Geminiani—a door that would never close.

Gem's outbursts were as famous as his feats on the bike.

RAPHAËL GEMINIANI

Born: June 12, 1925, in Clermont-Ferrand, France
Palmarès: French Championship 1953. Polymultipliée 1950 and 1951. Midi-Libre 1951. Bol d'Or des Monédières 1956, 1957, and 1958. Second in Tour de France 1951.

Hugo Koblet
The Pedaler of Charm

Hugo Koblet was a sort of deity lighting up the drab anonymity of the peloton. His class and good looks burst forth everywhere. For the elegance of his position on the bike, entertainer Jacques Grello baptized him "the Pedaler of Charm." Worshipped by the crowds, winner of the 1951 Tour de France, this Zürich native was becoming part of the Tour's romanticism, thanks to his seductive nature, when he was struck by a mysterious illness after returning from a visit to the Americas. The epic hero's imperial progress had suddenly lost its momentum.

His career was cut short, but what a career! He outshone all his rivals, and, in the words of Jean Bobet, when he arrived on the scene, "everything that cycling counted as grand suddenly seemed ridiculously small." A cruel fate awaited him. He, the prodigal child who breathed gentility and elegance, had never learned to deal with money and deceit. He failed to adjust to everyday life, and he died tragically when he drove his car into a tree. Did he deliberately take his own life? Or was he the victim of a true road accident? It seems more appropriate to remember the handsome Hugo as he appeared to the crowds, in the spotlight, throughout the early 1950s.

In 1950, at age twenty-five, almost without warning, he entered the closed world of the great road racers—indeed, he broke through the unyielding Italian coalition and became the first foreigner to win the Giro d'Italia. Then at the 1951 Tour de France, he played his trump card when it was least expected, on a broiling-hot July 15 in a seemingly unimportant stage between Brive and Agen. At kilometer 37, on the climb out of the Dordogne valley at Lanzac, he slipped away from the pack and launched one of the finest feats of bravery in Tour history. There he was, gone. By kilometer 75 at Pont-Carral, with more than 100 kilometers still to ride, his lead reached almost four minutes. The technical director of the Swiss team, Alex Burtin, remained with his racer all day, giving him advice as Koblet turned a gear of 52 x 16, which moved him 6.85 meters with every turn of the pedals. He rarely shifted to the fifteen-tooth sprocket. At one point, in a wind-battered passage, he lost a minute to his pursuers. His reply was phenomenal: 10 kilometers later his lead had returned to 3:35. Behind him the peloton was subdued, dazed. The finish line was before him. When he crossed it, his state of freshness was so evident that he even managed to click his excellent Swiss stopwatch to check his time gains. The peloton, which remained stunned by his exploit, didn't arrive until 2:35 later.

Koblet had no bad patches in that Tour. He took the leader's jersey in the Pyrenees, despite the presence of Fausto Coppi, Louison Bobet, Stan

Ockers, and Fiorenzo Magni, and never gave it up. His class and his superiority took on a humiliating appearance for the others. He remains a legend, even for the way in which, after crossing the finish line, he would comb his hair and wipe his face with eau de cologne—which, of course, was of the highest quality.

Hugo Koblet's stylish elegance was accompanied by a moral elegance. The Pedaler of Charm was a classy guy. It is rare among cyclists for racers to congratulate an opponent warmly and sincerely, but he took real pleasure in the success of a rival. The triumphs of others did not irritate him, even in the bad times that he later experienced. But his career was short. Victim of a pernicious venereal disease, Koblet never regained the effortless style for which he had been known. His pedaling became jerky, and glory turned its back on him. He did not deserve such a fate.

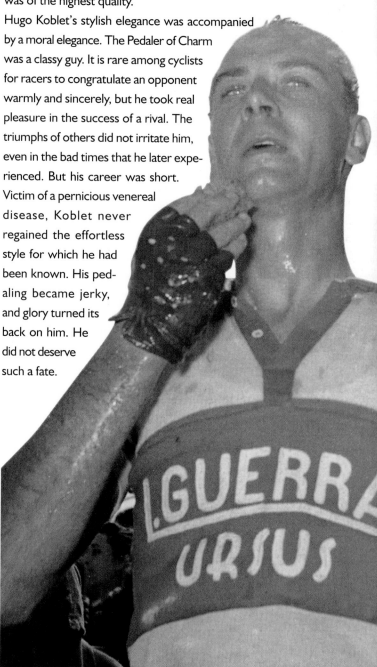

Even at the height of suffering, Koblet knew how to remain elegant. He was a prince.

HUGO KOBLET

Born: March 21, 1925, in Zürich, Switzerland
Died: November 6, 1964
Palmarès: Tour de France 1951. Giro d'Italia 1950. Tour of Switzerland 1950, 1953, and 1955. Tour de Romandie 1953. Grand Prix des Nations 1951.

Ferdi
Kubler
Cycling's Cowboy

Ferdi Kubler emerged from World War II as the great star of Swiss cycling. He had given an indication of his talent by winning Swiss championships in track pursuit, hill climbing, and cyclo-cross, and by breaking the Swiss hour record. A fine athlete, he was driven by a passion for winning that sometimes bordered on fanaticism. He had the sharp profile of an eagle and seemed permanently charged with electricity. French cyclists who had taken refuge in neutral Switzerland during the war had noted that this gaunt, birdlike rider could climb

and time-trial strongly, and could even outkick the fastest sprinters. Along with the temperament of a thoroughbred, he had a good sense of timing and consummate knowledge of race techniques. Though he shouted abuse at himself to gain motivation on the road, he also knew how to conserve his strength and deceive opponents with subtle tactics. His athletic qualities seemed most suited to the one-day classics, but his victory at the Tour of Switzerland in 1942 proved that he had the stuff of a complete road racer.

Nevertheless, he was not considered a good enough tactician to one day add his name to the palmarès of the Tour de France. He proved just the opposite in 1950, giving a standout performance after the incidents of the Pau–St. Gaudens stage—in which Gino Bartali was roughed up by some rowdy spectators and both of the Italian teams pulled out of the race. Once in the *maillot jaune*, Kubler buckled down as if by magic to vigorously defend his lead in the Alps and then stamped his authority on the race by winning the St. Étienne–Lyon time-trial stage.

Kubler's big year was 1951. He won Rome-Naples-Rome, the Tour de Romandie, and the Tour of Switzerland; he achieved a brilliant double at the Weekend Ardennais by winning Liège-Bastogne-Liège and Flèche-Wallonne (an exploit he repeated in 1952); and then he won the world road championship at Varese, Italy.

Kubler was timeless, and he is still as fiery today as he was at age twenty. Writing in *L'Équipe*, Jean Bobet said that Kubler treated each race like a Western—he had a way of neighing like a horse, grabbing his handlebars like a pair of pistols, and tossing his cap into the wind to make you think that he was the cowboy of cycling. "He did not want to have enemies," Bobet continued, "because he knew that victory is more easily handled among friends. Neither a schemer nor Machiavellian, he was a sort of modern Talleyrand in the art of provoking or destroying coalitions."

Kubler was capable of discussing French, Belgian, or Swiss francs, lire, or pesetas and of making the conversions while rolling along at 50 kilometers per hour. He was a smooth talker, ingratiating, insistent under certain circumstances, and generally obtained the alliances he sought. But when it came time to pay up, he was often struck with a sudden amnesia....

FERDI KUBLER

Born: July 24, 1919, in Marthalen-Adliswil, Switzerland
Palmarès: World Championship 1951. Tour de France 1950. Tour of Switzerland 1942, 1948, and 1951. Tour de Romandie 1948 and 1951. Rome-Naples-Rome 1951. Liège-Bastogne-Liège 1951 and 1952. Flèche Wallonne 1951 and 1952. Bordeaux-Paris 1953. Green jersey of Tour de France 1954.

One anecdote is enough to characterize Kubler. In the eleventh stage of the 1955 Tour de France, from Marseille to Avignon, he attempted one of those crazy attacks that were his hallmark. From the first slopes of Mont Ventoux, on a day of tropical heat, he attacked as if he were riding up a simple railway bridge. Raphaël Geminiani managed to go with him, though surprised by such recklessness, and had the time to throw out: "Easy Ferdi, the Ventoux is not a mountain like all the others." Kubler, superbly, replied in his broken French: "Ferdi too not like the others—Ferdi great champion!"

The 1950 Tour de France was Kubler's moment of glory. Here he's in the process of dropping Louison Bobet (below).

Greg LeMond
America Has Arrived!

When Cyrille Guimard, the wily *directeur sportif* of the Renault team, signed up an American racer by the name of LeMond, it was obvious from the beginning that the Frenchman had struck a good deal. But how unusual he was, this slender nineteen-year-old from Reno, Nevada. Most striking about this young rider as he moved through the amateur ranks was his virtuosity, his ease within the peloton. The Europeans came to ask themselves how an American could acquire such skills.

On the slopes of the Sierra Nevada, LeMond first became familiar with the joys of skiing and proved to be such an acrobat that he was enrolled in a school of hot-dog skiing. He always remembered the period when he took risks on the fresh snow. Yet, did anyone know that at age two, this little skier had had a kidney removed owing to a crushed artery? And how did he come to have a passion for cycling? It was a simple thing: A race passed in front of his house when he was fourteen years old. He liked what he saw and thought that this sport would be an excellent way to train for skiing. A year later he started his first bike race and won it—the first step toward glory.

At age eighteen Greg LeMond won the world junior road championship in 1979. Four years later he became the world professional road champion, winning the 270-kilometer race at Altenrhein, Switzerland, in a bold solo breakaway, displaying a remarkable state of physical freshness. This victory was a first compensation for a youth who had risked everything to succeed in his athletic career. His momentum was assured. To remain at the center of his profession, LeMond decided to move to Kortrijk, Belgium. Life would be easier there for his wife, Kathy, who from their new home was able to tune in to English television shows and so feel less alone while her champion husband was making a name for himself in European cycling. Everyone was convinced that this American, enterprising and audacious, hardworking and patient, would quickly reach a new level. He did

so in 1986, when he fulfilled a teenaged dream of winning the Tour de France. His victory was won with panache but was nevertheless troubled by the dubious attitude of his co-team leader, Bernard Hinault, throughout the three weeks. For instance, on the evening of the Alpe d'Huez stage, after LeMond and Hinault had brought the peloton to its knees and crossed the finish line hand in hand, the Frenchman said to his lieutenant in the *maillot jaune*: "Now you can relax; I won't attack anymore." What a surprise it was, then, for the leader of the Tour to hear Hinault declare on the next day, a rest day, "The Tour is not over...." Until the very end, his teammate left doubt over his intentions. But LeMond won his first Tour de France anyway.

Having finishing third and second at the two previous Tours, LeMond thus continued his perfect ascendancy by taking cycling's supreme prize at the age of twenty-five. But in early May 1987, news from across the Atlantic threw the European sports world into turmoil: LeMond had almost lost his life in a hunting accident. There would be no repeat performance at the Tour de France that year.

LeMond worked hard to recover from his shotgun wounds and eventually returned to the Tour to win twice more, most memorably in 1989, when the *Grande Boucle* experienced a sensational and dramatic conclusion. LeMond defeated Laurent Fignon by eight seconds—the narrowest gap ever recorded—to win an epic race. LeMond went on that summer to achieve a fabulous double by taking his second world pro championship at Chambéry, France.

LeMond was first and foremost the one who defeated Hinault and Fignon at the Tour de France.

GREG LEMOND

Born: June 26, 1961, in Lakewood, California
Palmarès: World Championship 1983 and 1989. Tour de France 1986, 1989, and 1990. Tour de l'Avenir 1982. Dauphiné Libéré 1983. Coors Classic 1981 and 1985. Tour DuPont 1992.

Jeannie
Longo
Sovereign and Eternal

In the image of Eddy Merckx, whose appetite for victory she shares, Jeannie Longo has a refined sense of her profession: She is an eternally dissatisfied perfectionist! She has brought to women's cycling the toughness it previously lacked,

marking the racing world with her exploits as much as her overpowering personality.

Jeannie Longo has always given the impression—and always confirmed—that she is multifaceted, that she is able to win in every discipline: on the road or on the track, in the mountains or against the clock, in sprinting or in the pursuit or points race. And always, in spite of the words that we could lavish upon her, her speech and her looks don't betray the flow of her thoughts, which pursue impervious and inaccessible directions.

She has been called aggressive, barely sociable. But looking at her impressive palmarès, we undoubtedly forget that all her success, on road and track, has been the fruit of her sacrifices during an adolescence that could have been more carefree. She wanted to be successful and to endure, to isolate herself from the turmoil of daily life, to master her potential in order to win everywhere and always.

And because she was alone in a masculine world while she carried female performance to new heights, she suddenly needed a shoulder to lean on. When she married Patrice Ciprelli, she found a husband and a coach who understood her, who knew that he had to allow his wife to advance along paths of hidden solitude and occasionally to intervene—sometimes firmly—to soften this "piece of a tempest," in Bismarck's words.

In 1986 a cycling magazine chose Longo as its "man of the year," a distinguished compliment in a sport where misogyny still has a strong hold. Three Tours de France Féminins, a dozen world titles, a series of world hour records, and victories on every continent punctuate her career, which was interrupted by a brief "retirement" in 1990. She returned in anticipation of the Olympic Games in Barcelona, where she reached an Olympic podium for the first time, but she had to wait for Atlanta in 1996, her fourth appearance at the Games, to finally take home an Olympic gold medal. In Sydney in 2000 she set out on yet another mission and took home a bronze medal in the time trial.

She continues to fight against media groups that show no interest in women's cycling; against cycling federation officials who try to impose their collective rule on her; and against her fellow competitors, who sometimes seem more determined to see her lose than to win themselves. All this lends a certain slant to her thoughts that sometimes prevents a smile from forming on her lips. "The best with the worst of characters" is how she has been described in the press.

On the track, on the road, for all time, Jeannie Longo (above, next to Maria Canins, her great rival in the Tour de France Féminin) has had just one concern: victory.

Independent, elusive, somewhat on the fringe of things, she was no doubt born that way back in 1958 at St. Gervais in the French Alps. Her family tells stories of how, at age five, she refused any help in learning to ride a bike. Even the priests did not manage to tame this puny, insolent kid. After all, where was God in all this? She excelled on skis and won championships at the university level. A fracture put an end to her skiing hopes, and she switched her athletic goals to cycling. We know what was to come....

Each year when winter whitens the peaks above Grenoble, the Ciprellis

return home. There Jeannie likes to spend her time preparing food or devoting herself to her favorite pastime: the piano. She also enjoys other domestic pleasures, such as caring for her rabbits, chickens, and geese.

When the buds of spring reappear, she returns to the battlefield of cycling, where intuition is not always present. She is able to protect herself because her experience has revealed that unusual alloys can produce elements of contradiction in the human soul. But she continues to move forward ... disconcerting, magnificent Jeannie.

JEANNIE LONGO

Born: October 31, 1958, at St. Gervais-les-Bains, France
Palmarès: Olympic Road Race Gold Medal 1996; Silver Medal 1992. World Road Race Champion 1985, 1986, 1987, 1989, and 1995. World Time-Trial Champion 1995, 1996, 1997, and 2001. Tour de France Féminin 1987, 1988, and 1989. World Hour Record (new standard) 2000 (45.094 km).

Luis
Ocaña
The Sun Is Dead

"Luis Ocaña perhaps wasn't intrinsically the best in the Tour, but he was its sun, while forming with the superstar himself a separable couple, whose complementary warmth and radiance dazzled us," wrote Antonin Blondin on July 13, 1971, after Ocaña's dramatic crash on the Menté Pass, which ended an epic battle-in-the-making with the "superstar," Eddy Merckx. The crash was one of many tragedies in the life and career of an endearing champion in the history of cycling.

A child of the postwar period, Luis Ocaña was born in the heart of New Castile, then moved at age twelve with his parents to southwestern France. He became a celebrity at the 1971 Tour de France, starting with his glorious climb toward Orcières-Merlette. On that stage—the eleventh—which started in Grenoble, Ocaña resolved to break the spirit of Eddy Merckx. The day before he had felt that the Belgian was a bit less fluid than usual, and he decided this time to test Merckx from the start. Upon the urging of the team director Raphaël Geminiani, the Portuguese rider Joaquim Agostinho was the first to break away on the difficult Laffrey climb. Ocaña took off in pursuit, followed by Joop Zoetemelk, Lucien Van Impe, and Gösta Pettersson, who all realized that this was a critical moment. Merckx, on the other hand, lost contact. It was a momentous moment.

There were still more than 100 kilometers to ride across an arid, shadeless landscape with an off-putting series of climbs, to which was added heat-wave weather—precisely the topographical and climatic conditions that favored Luis Ocaña. That day the Spaniard left a fantastic impression of power that emanated from his smooth pulls—no jerkiness disturbed his harmonious motion. You couldn't say the same about his breakaway

companions, who were arched over their bikes at every turn of the pedals. The paceline became more and more extended. Ocaña understood the situation and accelerated again, soon finding himself alone. At the foot of the Col du Noyer, Merckx had already fallen three minutes behind. Ocaña had 70 kilometers left to cover. He hung on.

Then they came to the rugged finishing climb to Orcières-Merlette. The Spaniard continued upward, out of reach in the summer light, as if deaf to the cheers of the crowds, who were welcoming a new giant of the road. At Orcières, an unbelievable result: The crowd had to wait 8 minutes, 42 seconds to see the arrival of Eddy Merckx, who had just suffered the heaviest loss of his career.

Alas, on the fourteenth stage, Revel-Luchon, a mountain storm of rare violence exploded over the Menté Pass. It was impossible to see even 5 meters ahead. "The Pyrenees were the prisoners of a dark marriage," wrote Paul Katz in *Paris-Jour.* In a few seconds the apocalypse was upon the riders. Enormous hailstones pounded down on the caravan, lashing and blinding the riders. The mountain rumbled and poured layers of silt across the road surface.

On the steep descent, wet brake pads were not working, and the racers had great difficulty just keeping upright. Suddenly, at a bend in the road, came the drama: Ocaña fell apart in the storm. What happened? No one saw the accident, but the most generally accepted version is that the Spaniard, having fallen trying to follow Merckx, was picking himself back up without too much trouble when Zoetemelk suddenly appeared and crashed violently into him. The Dutchman confirmed the story, saying that he lost control of his bike and hit Ocaña squarely in the chest. The Tour was over for the Castilian. Even though he emerged from the adventure with increased stature, this result did not console him. He was convinced that he would have won that Tour.

The Merckx-Ocaña duel never recurred. Ocaña was forced to withdraw in 1972 and didn't have to face Merckx in 1973. That race proved to be a Tour that the Spanish racer won with panache, dominating Bernard Thévenet, José-Manuel Fuente, Zoetemelk, and Van Impe.

Luis Ocaña was the embodiment of simplicity, generosity, and panache and loved his sport passionately. Luis was the sun. "He loved life so much that he preferred to give himself death," wrote Jean-Michel Rouet in the May 20, 1994, edition of *L'Équipe* after Ocaña committed suicide. The sun had set.

Luis Ocaña, the only champion who made
the incomparable Eddy Merckx falter and doubt.

LUIS OCAÑA

Born: June 9, 1945, in Priego, Spain
Died: May 19, 1994
Palmarès: Tour de France 1973. Vuelta a España 1970. Dauphiné Libéré 1970, 1972, and 1973. Grand Prix des Nations 1971. Baracchi Trophy 1971 (with Leif Mortensen).

when he was race leader heading into the last stage, Pingeon heard that the organizers wanted a more prestigious winner. A coalition was put together to give the victory to Tom Simpson, but the British rider blew a tire in the last kilometer, and it was the veteran Frenchman André Foucher who prevailed. At Paris-Nice in 1966, launched on a breakaway that had every chance of success, Pingeon was the victim of two punctures. His team car wasn't there to help him out. Bitter and disillusioned, he withdrew from the race. He was often seen falling prey to these rejections and being brought down by his moodiness; his continual worries over his vertebrae, sinuses, bronchial tubes; and even his pathological fear of hunger and cold.

Roger
Pingeon
The Misfortune of Virtue

Roger Pingeon had incomparable class, inversely proportional to his wavering morale. Like a meteor, he flashed through the skies of cycling, misunderstood by the public. He was a strapping six-footer, resembling a wading bird from the Camargue marshlands, and had a windbreaker of a nose. He totally embraced his sport, like a thoroughbred of the road. No one knew better how to meticulously study an itinerary, circumvent its traps, and adhere to a diet and regimen so stringent that even his own teammates were in disbelief.

He came from the Jura, a mountainous region along the Swiss border, where the people follow a strict moral code. He was shocked when he arrived in the professional peloton to see that he had ridden into a jungle that had its own laws and underhand ethics. A discreet, even secret person, he believed that destiny must be trying to persecute him. Undoubtedly, he was not completely wrong. For example, at the 1965 Midi Libre,

In 1967, through this daily labyrinth, he finally found a way to glory. For a couple of years the Tour de France was raced by national teams instead of the trade teams that contested the rest of the season's races. Three men had claim to the leadership of that year's French national team: Lucien Aimar, Raymond Poulidor, and Pingeon. At the start Poulidor noted Pingeon's impeccable physical condition. He was right. On the fifth stage Pingeon made a solo move to catch a breakaway group of twelve, dropped the group on the Mur de Thuin climb, in the Belgian Ardennes, and won the stage. He finished more than six minutes ahead of his main rivals and took the yellow jersey. Afterward the entire French team, including Poulidor, placed itself in his service. In trouble on the Galibier, Pingeon showed great courage as Poulidor paced him up the giant climb and allowed him to keep the *maillot jaune*—which he would guard all the way to Paris. The 1967 Tour was certainly his masterpiece.

Pingeon had the shrewdness and the class to resist Eddy Merckx (left page) as well as Raymond Poulidor and Jacques Anquetil (above).

ROGER PINGEON

Born: August 28, 1940, in Hauteville, France
Palmarès: Tour de France 1967 (second in 1969). Vuelta a España 1969. Polymultipliée 1967.

Roger Rivière
Broken Momentum

From the moment Roger Rivière began his cycling career as a track racer, the public understood that it was in the presence of a phenomenon. This conclusion was no mistake. Rivière quickly won fame and glory, accumulating world titles in the pursuit and breaking the world hour record. Having set himself apart, this elegant native of St. Étienne was virtually unbeatable on the track.

Coming from the closed but glorious world of velodromes, Rivière was afraid of what awaited him in professional road racing. He feared the crowds that were not quite the same, showing their fists like spectators at the circus, and he feared not being able to do justice to his quite legitimate ambitions. What the crowds saw was his ease on a bike, his detached air, and his great adolescent smile that some found disdainful. But he had an obsessive fear of disappointing people and above all of failing to defeat his great rival, Jacques Anquetil, who won the Tour de France the year Rivière turned pro. Their duel, exacerbated by the press, excited the crowds. When negative influences suggested that he adopt certain medicinal practices, Rivière didn't hesitate to follow this marginal path. He believed it would carry him to victory, but it was the beginning of his downfall....

On July 10, 1960, the long, multicolored ribbon that is the Tour de France unfurled through the hills of the Cévennes, over the Perjuret Pass—the name of which means "treacherous" in old French—and down the side of Mount Aigoual. As the clock struck twelve, Rivière misjudged a turn, crashed into a low wall, and plunged into a ravine. His race ended—in more senses than one— next to a tree that had lost its leaves, as if to welcome him onto a stretcher. But if the tree could one day retell the story, Roger Rivière would receive no laurels. The sin of pride had driven him to test himself on the descent against the Italian Gastone Nencini, at that time the best downhill rider in the world. In this game of skill, Rivière was bound to be the victim.

He began his tragic "rehabilitation" with great courage. There was a frail hope among those who treated him, but undoubtedly excessive hope around him and in the world in general, where everyone was suddenly

The most elegant of champions destroyed himself when he crashed into a ravine.

conscious that an exceptional human being was missing from the starting lineups. The press itself, which does not easily abandon its idols, became caught up in the game of prognostics, or even illusions. Rivière was shown trying hard to become himself again during his first dip in the healing waters of the hot springs at Lamalou, in the same Cévennes countryside that had seen him immobilized a short time before, an ancient land that had been so hard on humankind. He was photographed from all angles as he took his first steps as a disabled person. The public was making him march to its demands in every sense of the word.

In the end the public discreetly lowered the curtain on him. Rivière would bring his fans no more reason to hope. He sank deeper into the pages of current affairs and then brutally disappeared. What he was suffering in his ruined body was no longer of interest to the press. Soon he shut himself off from the world and sank into an abyss of despair. He was searching for an escape, an artificial paradise. He did not know that he was on first-name terms with something unbeatable. The drugs undoubtedly made him forget that life has its rules and its rigors. By defying the taboos, he opened the doors to a life of exile.

He was an invalid and suffered like a martyr. He became a drug addict—and was brought to justice—to get through the long path of suffering that lay ahead of him, a path that over time only became longer and more burdensome for his handicapped legs. The moral support of those who had made him the finest of champions had vanished.

As if to inflict one last punishment, this absurd destiny had the ultimate thrashing in store for him. He was so eroded by the cancers of the soul that the final blow—the real thing in the medical sense of the word—was simply a deliverance. Even at the end, the irony of it all remained a tragic joke…. He died on an April 1.

ROGER RIVIÈRE

Born: February 23, 1936, in St. Étienne, France
Died: April 1, 1976
Palmarès: World Pursuit Champion 1957, 1958, and 1959. Amateur Tour of Europe 1956. World Hour Record 1957 (46.923 km) and 1958 (47.346 km).

Jean
Robic
Leather Head

Jean Robic knew how to build a legend. He exercised a certain fascination over the public, for there was something extraordinary in his energy, his physical courage, and his morale. He was obstinate and pigheaded—never was there a better example of a stubborn Breton. *Vas-y* [Go], Robic!" He heard this affectionate encouragement all his life, from his victory in the 1947 Tour de France until his last Tour in 1959, when he was unceremoniously eliminated two days from the finish. He refused to suffer, just as he ignored defeat. This stoic face was usually the extent of what the public saw in him. Many were unaware that Robic had an inordinate passion for the bike and its mechanics. If he had put into practice all that he knew, the technology of the bicycle would have progressed at a stupefying rate. However, his most remarkable technical feat falls in the domain of the automobile: He once had to repair a complete gearbox in the middle of the night, alone on the road,

300 kilometers from Paris, and still managed to show up at the start of the French Championship some hours later in Montlhéry.

His greatest glory was his victory in the first Tour de France of the postwar period, in 1947. He wasn't a favorite, but he didn't steal the victory. Throughout the event he proved himself the most complete racer. He began with a stage win at Strasbourg, then dominated in the mountains.

He did not look like anyone else. ... He was so ugly that it made him handsome!

The man needed cycling, and each year he came to recharge his batteries with the same delight. In 1959, at the age of thirty-eight, he returned to the Tour de France. Bruised once more during the first stages on the cobblestones of the north, he continued. It seemed that he would make it to the Parc des Princes. Alas! He was eliminated two days before the finish. Dropped by the pack on the little Échalon Pass, above Oyonnax, he covered 170 kilometers alone to finally learn that he had been eliminated for finishing outside the time limit. Even so, he was given a lap of honor at the Parc and received a massive ovation that somewhat appeased his disappointment. Robic never went unnoticed, with his leather helmet, elephant ears, and wrinkled face. You either loved him or hated him, but his popularity was unparalleled. His seeming inability to know what he was saying was disconcerting, but in an instant he could become touchingly sincere, as the following anecdote confirms. While on a train, he met an elderly man who was ignorant of what his career as a cyclist really entailed. "He did not know what it meant to take a pull in the peloton," said Robic. "I told him, look at ducks when they are flying in a group. There is always one of them who is leading, and he then pulls to the side, passes back down the line, and then it's someone else's turn to move to the front. And we certainly all do what the [first] duck did, because it is difficult to always ride alone at the front, against the wind!" He who rode against the wind—such was Robic's destiny.

On the Luchon-Pau stage, he finished sixteen minutes ahead of the *maillot jaune,* René Vietto, but he was still eight minutes behind on overall time, with only a few stages to go. Robic believed so much in his destiny that he told his teammates, "It's not over yet; I can feel it—I'm unstoppable." This comment must have cost him several unkind thoughts, for at Vannes, three stages from the end, the gap was unchanged, and he was certainly the only one who still believed he could win. The Vannes–St. Brieuc stage, a 139-kilometer time trial, was a decisive one that would theoretically determine the identity of the overall winner, whoever that might be. Robic, cheered on by the delirious crowds of his region, finished second behind the Belgian Raymond Impanis and moved into third place overall, 2:58 behind Pierre Brambilla—who took the yellow jersey from Vietto.

The last stage was one for the history books: Robic broke away on the Bonsecours hill as the race left Rouen and caught up with Édouard Fachleitner, a member of the French national team. Brambilla was dropped, and Robic and Fachleitner finished together at the Parc des Princes in Paris, with Robic taking the overall victory.

Never again would he be in a position to win the Tour, but when Robic reached the twilight of his career he still wanted to keep going, despite being hurt by crashes that were always holding him back. He remained a character who left no one indifferent.

JEAN ROBIC

Born: June 10, 1921, in Condé-lès-Vouziers, France
Died: October 6, 1980
Palmarès: Tour de France 1947. Rome-Naples-Rome 1950. Tour de Haute-Savoie 1952. Polymultipliée 1952. World Cyclo-Cross Championship 1950.

Tom Simpson
Death in the Afternoon

Tom Simpson made the first turns of his pedals in the county of Yorkshire, which was then to England what Brittany is to France: a great source of good bike racers. Simpson, under the colors of the Union Jack, had already competed as a team pursuiter in the Melbourne Olympics when he decided, at age twenty-one, to embark on a professional career. As the United Kingdom did not offer much of a road-racing program, he was directed to Brittany, where he could make a living in the region's hundreds of village races. So he left for St. Brieuc with a suitcase, his wrist shaky but his goal firm: to become a great road racer. Already a world-class track racer, he quickly adapted to the fast, sprint-every-lap style of the Breton circuit races. One Sunday shortly after his Easter 1959 arrival, he won a race at La Chèze ... "but in an armchair," Jean Bobet wrote afterward.

The racers of Brittany, who believed that they made their own laws in their territory, made a strong effort to work together and put a check on the usurper. Nothing could be done, though. Tom won dozens of regional races and clinched a pro contract with the St. Raphaël team—and five months after landing on French soil he raced in the world pro road race championship and came in fourth!

His eruption into the international arena caused a revolution in the British newspapers, which soon started featuring this new star in columns that until then had been virtually closed to cycling. As his career progressed, the Tour de France showed his courage, the Tour of Flanders his opportunism, and Milan–San Remo his finishing speed. Everyone everywhere wanted to see this phenomenon who knew how to express himself with an Oxfordian elegance in the purest cycling jargon.

Simpson was ambitious—he had decided to become a true champion and had to suffer body and soul. He built up a palmarès. He starred in the classics, winning two, and in 1962 became the first British rider to wear the Tour de France yellow jersey (finishing sixth overall). Only the rainbow jersey seemed to elude him. Then came the 1995 world's at San Sebastian in Spain's Basque Country. On the hilly Lasarte circuit he made a strong move to join an early twelve-strong breakaway group with Germany's Rudi Altig. Circumstances supported the attackers, and the incessant rain favored a race of attrition. The energetic British racer, whose offensive spirit was accentuated by the

coma. The race doctor couldn't revive him. The autopsy revealed that he had taken some performance-enhancing substances. The death of a champion plunged the sports world into disarray and went to the root of the heated struggle against doping. But the days slipped away, and with them the public's conscious-ness of a prob-lem that still plagues the sport.

World champion in 1965 (left page), Simpson, with Jacques Anquetil, Rudi Altig, and Eddy Merckx (top left), incarnated the joy of life before he met his fatal end.

tough conditions, attacked from the lead group on the circuit's main climb with almost 50 kilometers remaining. Only Altig could go with him. With the rest more than three minutes behind, the German launched the final sprint, thinking Simpson would weaken, but the Brit came through in the last 50 meters to score a historic triumph. The most courageous rider had won the race and become Britain's first world professional road champion. Simpson, alas, would become the victim of his own great courage and ambition that he took to an extreme. He wanted to go fast; maybe too fast. What happened to him at the 1967 Tour de France, on the thirteenth stage, Marseille-Carpentras, on July 13? Within sight of the summit of Mont Ventoux, at the height of a heat wave and on the toughest of mountain climbs, we saw him falter, his eyes glazed. Completely out of steam, he fell a first time. He was helped back onto the saddle. But he fell again and went into a

TOM SIMPSON

Born: November 30, 1937, in Haswell, England
Died: July 13, 1967
Palmarès: World Championship 1965. Tour of Flanders 1961. Bordeaux-Paris 1963. Milan–San Remo 1964. Tour of Lombardy 1965. Paris-Nice 1967. Tour du Sud-Est 1960.

Jean Stablinski
The Rewarded Lieutenant

He was first called by his true name, Jean Stablewski. He had Polish parents but opted for French citizenship at age sixteen in order to race in the French national junior championship, then known as the Premier Pas Dunlop. His father, who died in World War II, would have been a great help in facilitating his son's passion, for his mother had not exactly been praying for her son's growing interest in cycling. It is even said that one day she picked up a hammer to break the racing handlebars that her son, "Jeannot," had mounted on his old clincher bike. Was she afraid of losing the only man who remained in the house?

Young Jean resented not having a father perhaps more than anyone and encouraged his mother to find a new husband. With the meager literary skills he had obtained in school, he wrote to the matrimonial section of a Polish newspaper. His efforts were rewarded: A candidate presented himself. He was handsome and had a good job. Madame Stablewski remarried. The story could have stopped there. But a new life began, and Jean found that the events to follow were equally happy: his stepfather had not come alone. He had a daughter named Genia. She became Mrs. Jean Stablinski. Yes, by this time Stablewski—unpronounceable for the French—had turned to Stablinski under

the pens of local journalists, who were beginning to appreciate the qualities of this rider from the North who was never afraid to attack. They identified in him a natural ease with race tactics, which he initially used in the service of others. However, he was never considered a true *domestique* but rather a lieutenant, especially for Jacques Anquetil and André Darrigade on the French national team at the Tour de France. Stablinski had the double mission of helping the first and preparing the sprints of the second. In this capacity he was considered the ideal teammate.

But Stablinski, well aware of his athletic abilities, had no wish to risk conducting a career as an auxiliary, honorable as the role was. He decided from time to time to ride for himself. After winning the Paris-Valenciennes semiclassic and the Tour du Sud-Est stage race, he scored a brilliant victory in the 1958 Vuelta a España. He then showed an aptitude for circuit races. In these events, where the difficulties are repeated on each lap, "Stab," a masterful tactician, learned even the slightest details of the course in order to measure out his efforts with maximum precision. He knew that the repetition of the hills, descents, and turns had the effect of draining one's will, whereas his own was reinforced. He understood the mechanics of this type of course, multiplying his attacks, working hard in the breakaways, and pacing himself as the race evolved. Thus, he became the specialist of the French national championship, which he won four times, on the circuits at Reims, Les Essarts (near Rouen), Revel, and Châteaulin.

He won the supreme reward in 1962 by taking the world road championship at Salo, Italy, on the banks of Lake Garda. Stablinski had arrived for the world's straight from the Three Sister Cities race in Belgium, which he won on a very selective circuit. How would he make an impact on a course like that in Salo, with the Taormina Wall and its 12-percent grade? He moved ahead after 100 kilometers, and with 196 kilometers still to race, he was riding with Seamus Elliott, Jos Hoevenaers, Franco Balmamion, and Joseph Groussard. The Irishman Elliott made a solo break with just 20 kilometers to go, but Stablinski was feeling strong too. He left the others behind, caught up to his friend Seamus—his opponent in this case—and, despite a puncture, rode away from Elliott with the finish in sight. A job well done.

Stab, the favorite lieutenant of Jacques Anquetil, wore the jersey of a French champion on four occasions.

JEAN STABLINSKI

Born: May 21, 1932, in Thun–St. Amand, France
Palmarès: World Championship 1962. Vuelta a España 1958. French Championship 1960, 1962, 1963, and 1964. Paris-Brussels 1963. Tour of Belgium 1965. Paris-Luxembourg 1965. Grand Prix of Frankfurt 1965. Amstel Gold Race 1966. Baracchi Trophy 1965 (with Jacques Anquetil).

Roger
Walkowiak
The Unpardonable Omission

This is the simple story of a man from the Marais neighborhood, in the city of Montluçon, in the center of France. The story of a little metal lathe-turner turned pedal-turner in the Tour de France. Roger Walkowiak didn't seemed destined for glory. It almost seemed that he was born with a spirit of denial, so quick was he to use his physical strength to enhance the glory of others. Within cycling circles, the specialists who formed the teams quickly spotted him. The French national team at the Tour de France needed a kid who wouldn't turn up his nose at any task. Walkowiak was the perfect *domestique*, but the strange finger of fate diverted him at the last minute before the 1956 Tour, which saw him ride for the Nord-Est-Centre regional squad. Perhaps destiny had a different goal for him; maybe it wanted to cast its malicious spell

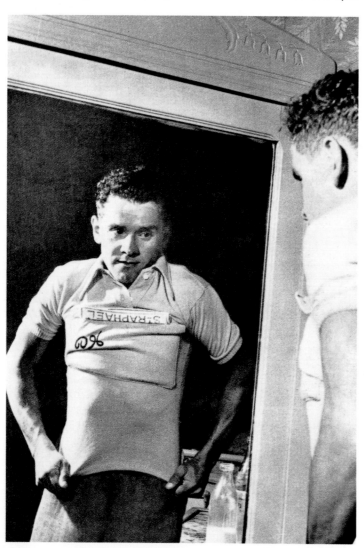

and carry him into the torment of glory—he who dreamed only of riding comfortably in the peloton from which he could applaud his friends, always better off than he. At least, that was what he thought.

Indeed, the strange hand of destiny came knocking one day…. On the Tour's seventh stage from Lorient to Angers, he slid into a breakaway that included some twenty men. He did his full share of the work as the group began gaining minute after minute. In the peloton, the Belgian and French national teams were working against each other and eventually gave up the struggle. The regional racer from Montluçon reaped the benefits. On a beautiful July afternoon, "Walko" became the new *maillot jaune*. He quietly accepted this gift from heaven, tried on his new yellow tunic, and looked at himself in the mirror. In the end, he thought, he was no more ridiculous than the others. He pledged that evening to defend his lead for as long as he could. Really, to keep it for two or three days would be true glory. But someone else was thinking for him: his *directeur sportif*, Sauveur Ducazeaux. Between eating a pear from Maine-et-Loire and some cheese from Deux-Sèvres, the team boss suddenly told him: "Roger, I think you can win the Tour de France!"

We must excuse this would-be *domestique* for hardly listening to his director that evening, especially as he was asking him to intentionally lose his *maillot jaune*. At first Roger turned a deaf ear, but even so the words were melodious. He had been commanded to give up the trophy in order to … take it back when the time came, for it was evident from that point on that he had the ability to do so.

So he listened. The jersey was gone after two days. Roger became anonymous once more but armed, this time, with exorbitant ambition. Under orders from Ducazeaux, he waited as the peloton crossed the Garonne River, climbed over the Pyrenees, and promenaded through the ancient vineyards of Hérault and Provence before hitting the alpine peaks. Ducazeaux had decided to set up Roger's ambush there. The coup was successful. At Grenoble, Walkowiak was again wearing the yellow jersey. He raced toward his apotheosis, the Parc des Princes and the final victory. But he was not finished with his anonymity. The press began to savagely destroy his success: Walko had won his Tour on the flat stages … this was no champion. Roger alone knew that he had triumphed because he had been present in every important breakaway. The name Walkowiak, the "assassinated" *maillot jaune*, would receive no more attention than a single line in the library of cycling. A pity. This man deserved neither silence nor omission.

Since 1956 it is as if we bear a grudge against Walko for having won the Tour.

ROGER WALKOWIAK

Born: March 2, 1927, in Montluçon, France
Palmarès: Tour de France 1956. Second in Tour de l'Ouest 1952. Second in Paris–Côte d'Azur 1953. Second in Dauphiné Libéré 1955

THE WINGED GODS

hough the Tour de France remains wildly popular for its spectacular breakaways across the plain, its frenzied sprints, and its often dramatic time trials, the race possesses a single crown jewel: the mountains. The mountain passes enhance the Tour with a heavenly aura and heated competition. When the road begins to climb, higher and higher, the racer sees himself for what he is: alone against an implacable, granite-hard enemy.

The climber is the one who battles the mountain and whose actions, pushed to their extreme, take the spectator to the heart of an athlete's suffering. It is a special type of human being we come to encourage on these evil slopes, and there has never been a winner of the Tour who has not felt the push of wings on the decisive day. The mountain is a required enslavement, the link between heaven and earth, like a justice of the peace among all the warriors. It is in the mountains that cycling literally reaches its highest summits.

Lance
Armstrong
The Condemned Man
Who Escaped

To the general public, Lance Armstrong has become a hero. The crowds have followed him, incredulous and filled with wonder. What he has achieved is miraculous. He has conquered cancer, conquered the Tour de France.... Henceforth he will be regarded as a complete athlete, but there's a tendency to forget that he has been through hell. *He* doesn't want to forget. Armstrong has emerged stronger from an ordeal that should have killed him. "Each day that I am alive," he maintains, "is a victory over death." He likes to make himself suffer to remember this. He became tougher and cursed those who tried to minimize his struggle. To show them that the first victory was not a thing of chance, he won a second Tour de France, then a third....

For him there was a chasm of pain between the first great European picture that we have of him—finishing second at the Championship of Zürich in August 1992—and his first victory at the Tour de France, in July 1999.

He was not yet twenty-one when he signed his first professional contract with the Motorola team after competing at the Barcelona Olympics. His first pro event was the World Cup race at San Sebastian—he came in last. Then he went to Switzerland's World Cup classic in Zurich. He was runner-up to Viatcheslav Ekimov despite not having much tactical finesse. At Motorola, though, he had good mentors in his experienced teammates Phil Anderson and Sean Yates, and he learned to overcome his physical and tactical recklessness. With his solid build and huge ambition, he debuted at the Tour de France in 1993 and at Verdun became the event's youngest stage winner in fifty years. A month later, in a downpour at Oslo, he was crowned world professional road champion after slipping away from the heavy favorites Miguel Indurain, Olaf Ludwig, and Johan Museeuw. Armstrong went on to win the San Sebastian classic (1995), the Flèche Wallonne (1996), and the Tour DuPont (1995 and 1996)—performances that didn't escape the attention of Cyrille Guimard, *directeur sportif* of a new French team, Cofidis. When the Motorola team disbanded at the end of 1996, he signed Armstrong as his leader for the next season. Guimard is rarely mistaken about a man, particularly a fighter.

Armstrong returned to the United States in September. Then, just after his twenty-fifth birthday, he began experiencing some physical problems. When he spat up blood in his kitchen sink, he decided to find out what was wrong. After extensive tests at St. David's Hospital in his hometown of Austin, Texas, on October 2, 1996, a concerned Dr. Reeves invited him to take a seat. He wanted to speak to him tactfully but did not hide anything: Lance was suffering from testicular cancer, which had spread to his abdomen and his lungs and had just reached his brain. The doctor told him that his chance of survival was only 50 percent. The Texan was visibly affected. It was a total shock. Until that point in his life he had succeeded at almost everything he had tried; he felt invincible. Suddenly everything was falling apart. He no longer knew where he was going; he thought he was going to die. Yet he had a remarkable calmness, and his morale quickly returned. There was no time to lose; the doctors had to operate. The malignant testicle was removed, and on October 24 he underwent brain surgery at the University Medical Center in Indianapolis, followed by three months of chemotherapy. Between sessions he rode his bike again, maybe thirty to forty minutes at a time....

And the miracle took place. In October 1997, the doctors told him that he was clear of all malignancy—the cancer was gone. Would he have the confidence to return to cycling? This question was first answered in February 1998, in Andalusia, at the Ruta del Sol. Lance's reflexes responded and he finished the five-day race in good shape. At Paris-Nice, though, he cracked in a rainstorm on the second day and retired from the race. Psychologically, he wasn't ready. He finally returned to Europe in June—and won the Tour of Luxembourg. That victory perhaps had little importance for the general public, but it was enormous for Armstrong. He was ready. He ended the year with fourth place at the Vuelta a España, followed by two fourth-place finishes at the world championships.

LANCE ARMSTRONG

Born: September 18, 1971, in Plano, Texas
Palmarès: World Championship 1993. USPRO Championship 1993. Tour de France 1999, 2000, and 2001. Tour of Luxembourg 1998. Tour of Switzerland 2001. Dauphiné Libéré 2002. Midi Libre 2002. Clasica San Sebastian 1995. Flèche Wallonne 1996. Grand Prix des Nations 2000. Tour DuPont 1995 and 1996. GP Eddy Merckx 2000 (with Viatcheslav Ekimov).

Johan Bruynel, the new *directeur sportif* of the U.S. Postal Service team that Armstrong had joined after being abandoned by Cofidis, persuaded him that he could do no less than win the Tour de France in 1999. Lance took the yellow jersey by winning the prologue of the Puy-du-Fou on the Fourth of July. In the time-trial stage at Metz a few days later, he dominated once again, and then, beneath gloomy skies at Sestriere, he won the great mountain stage—and the Tour de France. He was not satisfied,

Lance Armstrong's story is that of a man miraculously cured who raced, in yellow, toward an incredible destiny.

though. In 2000 he did it again, confirming his status as the best time trialist and then proving in dramatic fashion that on a good day, no climber could match him. In 2001 he won the three toughest mountain stages and took a third Tour title. The condemned man had definitively escaped.

Federico
Bahamontes
The Eagle of Toledo

At first he was concerned only with being the virtuoso of mountain climbing. Spain's Alejandro Federico Martin Bahamontes was crowned King of the Mountains six times at the Tour de France, twice at the Vuelta a España, and once each at the Giro d'Italia and Tour of Switzerland. He was little known when he appeared at the start of the Tour de France in 1954—his first season as a professional—although he had just placed second in his own Vuelta a España. The French public knew nothing about how he sold fruit and vegetables at the market in Toledo so he could save enough pesetas to buy his first racing bike and line up at the city's grand prix. His country was then feeling the need of some positive heroes capable of healing the rifts and misunderstandings left by the Spanish Civil War.

Bahamontes answered the call, earning the public's admiration. Cities everywhere, from Toledo to Madrid, Salamanca to Albacete, Aranjuez to Avila, crowned him King of the Mountains. In light of all these performances, the Spanish national team manager did not hesitate in selecting him for the Tour de France. Federico was first over the great summits of the Pyrenees and the Alps and took his first title of best climber. It was the beginning of a long series. In 1957, in an editorial in *L'Équipe,* the paper's editor Jacques Goddet baptized him the "Eagle of Toledo." His portrait could have been like many painted by El Greco, another celebrity of Toledo—a face hollowed by suffering, the eyes widened by fear.

As he became familiar with Europe's great mountains, Bahamontes found himself flanked by another climber, a Luxembourg native closed as an oyster and skittish as a horse: Charly Gaul, the Angel of the Mountains. It was an appropriate title. One never climbed without the other. And Federico, like Charly, ultimately had it in him to win the Tour de France. In 1959 the Tour included a time-trial ascent of the Puy de Dôme, which began at 400 meters (1,312 feet) and climbed to 1,415 meters (4,642 feet) over a distance of 12.5 kilometers. Bahamontes gave a brilliant performance, perhaps the most impressive ever seen on the slopes of this extinct volcano in the Auvergne. That win helped him become the first Spaniard to win the Tour de France.

"I think," wrote Jean Bobet, "that if the young Bahamontes had been French—or Belgian or Italian—it would not have taken until 1959 for him to win the Tour de France. He had the class that distinguishes those of high pedigree. He did not know that bike racing is made not only of episodic exploits but also of calculations in the noblest sense of the term." In his defense, we can add that Bahamontes did not have a great team

to help him. So how did he manage to win the Tour? Fede pulled it off by placing himself in key attacks, moving in contention with his Puy de Dôme victory, and then taking the *maillot jaune* after a long breakaway with Gaul in the Alps.

As for his physical strength, he was exceptionally endowed—even beyond the ordinary. His constitution proved, to some extent, comparable to that of Fausto Coppi. His heart rate was slower than average, although he suffered from some arrhythmia. He had the emaciated face of the dead Gitano sung by the other Federico (playwright Federico García Lorca), but this cyclist was very much alive and entered the inner circle of Spain's greatest celebrities.

FEDERICO BAHAMONTES

Born: July 9, 1928, in Santo Domingo, Spain
Palmarès: Tour de France 1959. Spanish Championship 1958. Circuit Provençal 1965. Tour du Sud-Est 1965. Tour of Asturias 1955 and 1957. Best climber of the Tour de France 1954, 1958, 1959, 1962, 1963, and 1964.

Federico Bahamontes was the first Spaniard to win the Tour de France, in 1959.

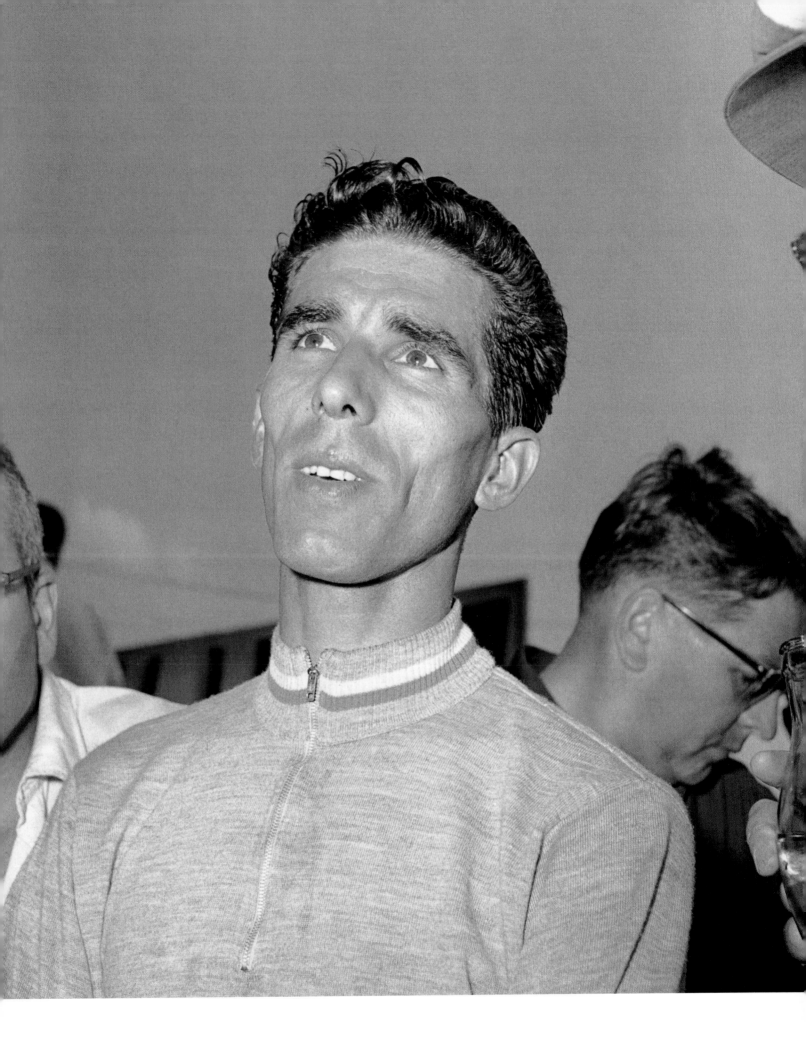

Pedro Delgado
Enshrouded Triumph

At the start of the 1988 Tour de France, Pedro Delgado was among those favored to win for two essential reasons. First, his role in 1987 as the heir apparent to winner Stephen Roche gave him a preemptive right over all the others. Losing a Tour de France by 40 miserable seconds generates a formidable desire for revenge, all the more so because at the 1987 Tour the Irishman had certainly not outclassed Delgado. On the scorching time-trial stage up Mont Ventoux, for example, Delgado had finished ahead of Roche.

In 1988 Delgado had prepared himself for the Tour as never before. Within the Spanish team, Reynolds, he carried an authority that had not been seen in him before. At the start of the *Grande Boucle,* he seemed to enjoy a certain aloofness among the announced favorites. The fight for the *maillot jaune*—which he had lost in the final time trial a year earlier—promised to show still more of the character of this Castilian, who was so gentle that he seemed lethargic. Since 1986 he had been the subject of a bidding war between the top European teams. Thus, after two years with the Dutch squad, PDM, he returned to Reynolds, with whom he had debuted in 1982. In Spain the fans swore by him, for none of his national rivals could match his all-around ability: Alvaro Piño seemed too inconsistent, Pello Ruiz-Cabestany was too limited in the mountains, Juan Gorospe did not live up to all the hopes placed in him, and Marino Lejarreta was at the end of his career.

In this 1988 Tour Delgado began raising eyebrows in the Besançon-Morzine stage. After French favorite Jean-François Bernard blew up, the other leaders moved to the front: Delgado but also Charly Mottet, Luis Herrera, Andy Hampsten, Erik Breukink, Urs Zimmermann, Steven Rooks, Gert-Jan Theunisse, and the Colombian Fabio Parra. As for Laurent Fignon, he was among those who had fallen back on the descent of the Pas-de-Morgins, the mountain pass that connects Switzerland and France, before climbing the little Col du Corbier. Here Parra suddenly launched a violent, unexpected attack. Among those most active in his pursuit was Delgado. What we admired in the Spaniard was his smart sense of tactics. He would stay in control of a difficult situation, knowing how to assess the

strength of his opponents like the most perceptive leader, allowing whomever he wished to get away or able to contain the attack of someone he deemed too dangerous. His astute riding on the Corbier was the first demonstration of these skills by the rider from Segovia, one that passed unnoticed by most observers but was very telling of his superb form. The Tour had really only just begun. But was it already moving toward a decisive phase on the thirteenth stage, a selective uphill time trial from Grenoble to Villard-de-Lans that finished at a ski resort above the town? The winner of the stage was none other than Delgado. The last to finish, he pulverized Bernard's time by 44 seconds. Happy with his performance, the Castilian headed over to take his drug test. From there another story would soon unfold.

In the Pyrenees Delgado's dominance was seen dramatically on the mountaintop finishes at Guzet-Neige and Luz-Ardiden, where thousands of Spaniards had crossed the border to cheer on their beloved Perico, unaware that a brewing storm would start to break over the Tour the next evening. After the crowds quietly left the Circuit du Lac in Bordeaux following the seventeenth stage, a first inkling of the scandal came to light. The French television station Antenne 2 let it be known that Delgado had tested positive in a drug test. The next day at noon the news was made official, but everyone was waiting for the results of a second blind test. This answer came that very night— the Spaniard was cleared by the international jury of commissaires. What provoked a certain annoyance was that there certainly was a trace of a suspicious substance in the first analysis: probenicid, a diuretic that masks the presence of anabolic steroids. Certainly it was a nondoping product, but it was one that the International Olympic Committee (but not cycling's UCI) had just placed on its list of prohibited substances because its presence suggests an intake of other drugs that one is attempting to mask. Be that as it may, Delgado had saved his *maillot jaune* and won his Tour de France.

PEDRO DELGADO

Born: April 15, 1960 in Segovia, Spain.
Palmarès: Tour de France 1988. Tour of Spain 1985 and 1989. Tour of Burgos 1991. Setmana Catalana 1993.

Pedro Delgado's victory in the 1988 Tour would have been so much sweeter without the rumors of doping.

Charly
Gaul
The Angel Exterminator

Charly Gaul was a phenomenon. He devoured mountain climbs in a syn-copated pedaling style, always on a "granny" gear ratio. Whoever saw this Luxembourg native climb laid eyes on what represents the best, the most beautiful, and the most heavenly of climbers.

He was a strange character. He didn't like to laugh or cry, didn't appre-ciate reporters and photographers, and could not bear heat. Did he like foul weather? We could answer in the affirmative, given that he per-formed his finest exploits in rain and snow. However, we could also make the point that in heat-wave conditions he won a time-trial stage of the 1958 Tour de France up the scorching slopes of Mont Ventoux that threw him into third place on general classification—and put him in a position to win the race.

In this Tour Gaul first proved his dominance in a time trial at the end of the first week. The day before this stage, which would take place over 46 kilometers on the selective Aulne circuit at Châteaulin, defending champion Jacques Anquetil had predicted, "He who wins tomorrow will win the Tour de France." The forecast proved exact. The circuit agreed with the Luxembourger, and Anquetil was forced to admit defeat, los-ing by seven seconds.

That year's Tour was replete with spectacular twists and turns. Raphaël Geminiani was constantly setting the race alight and took over the yellow jersey in the Pyrenees. Federico Bahamontes showed his determination by winning the fourteenth stage, Pau-Luchon, but Gaul emerged supreme on Mont Ventoux. However, it was too early to place all bets on him. The next day, on the Carpentras-Gap stage, he conceded 11 minutes to Geminiani and Anquetil. Then, on the road from Gap to Briançon, Bahamontes staked a claim by mastering the Izoard climb and winning the stage.

It would all change radically the next day, on a stage over five alpine climbs between Briançon and Aix-les-Bains. At the start an icy rain greeted the riders as they left their hotels. The conditions remained oppressive and sinister for all the riders except Charly Gaul, the champion of storms. The Luxembourger became a veritable "assassin." Without getting out of the saddle, he spun his small gears, playing with the opposition over the mountain passes of the Chartreuse, oblivious to the cold rain that never stopped falling. An exceptional climber, Gaul left everyone gasping on this apocalyptic stage. He crossed the finish line at Aix, almost 8 minutes ahead of runner-up Jan Adriaenssens, 10 minutes up on Vito Favero, and almost 15 in front of *maillot jaune* Geminiani.

Favero took over the leader's jersey, but his ownership was only temporary. Two days later Gaul won the 74-kilometer time-trial stage from Besançon to Dijon and became the undisputed winner of a Tour that had kept all of France on the edge of its seat. The *Grande Boucle* had finally smiled on Charly Gaul on his sixth participation.

Besides this success at the Tour de France, another exploit that brought him glory was his first victory at the Giro d'Italia, in 1956. When it seemed that he had lost the race, he sud-denly found himself back in his elements—the mountains and the cold—on Monte Bondone. In a torrent of rain and snow, his wheels were slipping, but no one could keep up with him. He was half frozen when he reached the summit. They wrapped him in a blanket like an infant, but his face was ageless. He remained in the leader's pink jer-sey all the way to Milan, to pull off a victory in legendary style.

Two years later he defeated Anquetil at the Giro but had to concede the Frenchman's dom-inance at the Tours of 1961 and 1962 before going quietly into retirement. Had Gaul loved this sport? Though he did not seem to make any par-ticular bond with it, he had served it elegantly, and we cannot but think that with a stronger national team than the ragtag Luxembourg outfit, he would have won more than just one Tour de France.

Gaul put on dominant climbing demonstrations to twice win the Giro d'Italia, in 1956 and 1959 (left page), but he was forced to submit to the law of Anquetil at the Tour de France in the early 1960s (below).

CHARLY GAUL

Born: December 8, 1932, in Asch, Luxembourg
Palmarès: Tour de France 1958. Giro d'Italia 1956 and 1959. Circuit des Six Provinces 1954. Tour du Sud-Est 1955. Tour of Luxembourg 1956, 1959, and 1961.

Luis Herrera
Colombian Defiance

In Colombia cycling is the most popular sport. Behind the scenes the government supports this passion, and in the center of Bogotá illuminated signs project the slogan, "Sport is life, drugs are death." The racing quality was high in Colombia's various cycling tours, even though the riders had a lot to learn about riding safely in a peloton.

Things changed after Colombian racers arrived in Europe in the early 1980s. When they returned to their country, they took with them a savoir-faire that rubbed off on the other racers. One of them was Luis Herrera, who became the first Colombian to win a stage of the Tour de France (l'Alpe d'Huez in 1984) and was hailed as a national hero.

Born on May 4, 1961, in Fusagasuga, barely an hour from Bogotá, Herrera felt disoriented when he lined up at the start of his first Tour de France in 1984. He managed to survive the first week on the flats, then took second place on the one difficult stage in the Pyrenees. He showed his true potential in the Alps with a second place to overall winner Laurent Fignon in an uphill time trial before he won the Alpe d'Huez stage. Herrera faded after that, but the journalists awarded him the distinction of an "au revoir," which means "until the next time." We saw him next, the following year, in a different light during his second encounter with the Tour, when he captured stage wins at Avoriaz and St. Étienne, to finally take home the trophy of best climber. He had certainly reached a new level, but his fragile physique remained a significant source of worry, and the end of his 1985 season was thwarted by tendinitis of the ankle. In 1986 Herrera's season was greatly anticipated, all the more so

because his team had acquired a new *directeur sportif*, the colorful Raphaël Geminiani. The Tour de France, which Herrera had made his main objective, was particularly mountainous that year, and Herrera was rightly placed among the pre-race favorites. Bernard Hinault knew this—so he made the race extremely demanding over the first half, putting the Colombians on the defensive and condemning them to a secondary role. Even Herrera couldn't find his best physical condition. It was time for another change. The sponsors of the Colombian team made an appeal to a former glory of their national cycling, Rafael Niño, to put the team back on track. He took a leave of absence from his medical work to implement a more effective structure to the team. He put Herrera through a series of sophisticated tests at Bogotá's sports medicine center, and the results confirmed both the rider's fragility and a certain slowness in his recovery time. The new directeur sportif established a low-profile racing schedule for Herrera, but then the rider was unexpectedly forced to compete at the Vuelta a España as a replacement for Fabio Parra. "Lucho" tackled the event with only fifteen or so days of racing in his legs, a severely reduced training regimen, and a complete lack of ambition because the races he had

Lucho had wings as soon as the road began to climb (above). And he made Hinault grimace at the 1985 Tour (left page).

ridden in Colombia had seen him regularly finish at the back of the field. A miracle occurred, though: Herrera won that Tour of Spain, picking up the great Lagos de Covadonga stage along the way. For the first time a non-European had won the Vuelta. He owed his victory to his climbing abilities, certainly, but also to his sense of the race and his remarkable resistance to foul weather. In the Tour de France that followed, Herrera earned his second King of the Mountains title, having hounded Stephen Roche, Charly Mottet, Laurent Fignon, and Pedro Delgado for three weeks. For Colombia it was even more than an athletic victory: It was a success that embodied the honor of a whole nation.

LUIS HERRERA

Born: May 4, 1961, in Fusagasuga, Colombia
Palmarès: Vuelta a España 1987. Dauphiné Libéré 1988 and 1991. Clasico RCN 1984 and 1986. Tour of Aragon 1992. Best climber of Tour de France 1985 and 1987.

Marco
Pantani
The Pirate

Marco Pantani has the meager physique of an explosive climber—a rider for whom each turn of a mountain road is a ramp from which he can launch himself toward the next summit. When he sets his climbing machine in motion, he is almost impossible to follow.

As if reflecting his biorhythms, he exploded onto the international scene at the 1994 Giro d'Italia, when he won the two great Dolomite stages in the same weekend and finished second overall. We awaited his appearance at the Tour de France. Confirmation: he climbed up on the podium with a third-place finish. Italy had found its latest star. At the following year's Tour, he won the Alpe d'Huez and Guzet-Neige stages, and later that year he propelled himself onto another podium—this one at the world road championship in Colombia alongside Abraham Olano, the winner, and Miguel Indurain. The Italians continued to sing his praises and prepared to write about the new legend of cycling. Unfortunately, destiny had something else in store for Pantani. After the world championship he crashed head-on into a car on a descent in the Milan-Turin race. The outcome: a double fracture of the tibia and the fibula. His cycling career was considered over. He was only twenty-five.

He recovered slowly. He was the only one to believe in his ability to return. With a rare will, he gradually returned to a normal life. Luciano Pezzi, a former *gregario* of Coppi who later directed Felice Gimondi to victory in the 1964 Tour de France, arrived opportunely at his side. Pezzi knew about Pantani's strong will but did not suspect the greatness of his spirit. After a bone graft in a rehabilitation center, Pantani began to feel his health creeping back. He would be a bike racer again. Even better, Pezzi told him that one day he would win the Tour de France and the Giro d'Italia. To back up his claims he offered Pantani a three-year contract with Mercatone Uno, the team for which Pezzi worked as head of public relations. Pantani left his crutches behind and took to the road again in August 1996. Pezzi also worked hard. He proposed to the team directors that they make the new recruit the exclusive leader. It was a huge gamble, but everyone agreed to go ahead. From that point, the rider who wore the

bandana wrapped around his shaven head, inspiring the nickname of "the Pirate," had big dreams.

Those dreams became reality. Three years after his terrible accident Pantani, the unstoppable climber, completed the double, just as Pezzi had predicted: He won both the Giro and the Tour in 1998. At the Giro, he began battling from the start at Nice, attacked in the Abruzzi, and proved his dominance on the summit of Piancavallo. This effort was not enough, though. Switzerland's Alex Zülle took over the pink jersey in a long time trial and pulled almost four minutes ahead of Pantani. Four decisive high-mountain stages remained. On the first, racing through the Dolomites, the Pirate made a blistering attack on the Marmolada climb. Zülle was left behind, but Pantani still had 50 kilometers left to the stage end in Val Gardena. He climbed the Passo Sella in a daze, but behind him Zülle had fallen apart. Pantani donned the first pink jersey of his career. He had done much more than turn around the Giro in his favor; he had reinstated the dream, the imaginary one at the heart of cycling, winning by means of a grand attack though the mountains.

The Tour de France loomed ahead. Pantani struggled in the first week, but a stage win in the Pyrenees pulled him into shooting range of race leader Jan Ullrich, and he delivered the body blow in the Alps, on the stage to Les Deux-Alpes. Through driving rain on the mighty Galibier, 5.5 kilometers from the summit and 48 kilometers from the stage finish, Pantani made two accelerations, then a solid attack. Ullrich gave up in one fell swoop.

From that point on, no challenge in cycling seemed too big for Pantani. It seemed that nothing could stop him. But then the image of the brilliant climber that he had built with his solo breakaways through the high mountains suddenly fell apart. Two days from the end of the 1999 Giro, which he had dominated and was set to win, a surprise blood test revealed that his hematocrit level was elevated far beyond the legal limit. Pantani won no honors that year. Wounded by accusations of having used questionable substances, he sank into a silence from which we wondered if he would ever emerge. Because he owed everything to

cycling and to the fans who still believed in him, he eventually started training again. He plunged back into depression but finally reemerged to show his class at the 2000 Tour de France, winning the twelfth stage on the summit of Mont Ventoux, and the fifteenth stage at Courchevel. All Italy was stamping its feet with joy. Until the next crazy act … whether sane or insane.

In pink or in yellow, Marco Pantani has climbed all the paths of glory.

MARCO PANTANI

Born: January 13, 1970, in Cesenatico, Italy
Palmarès: Giro d'Italia 1998. Tour de France 1998 (third in 1994 and 1997). Tour of Murcia 1999.

Bernard Thévenet
Way up There at Pra-Loup

When Bernard Thévenet competed at his first Tour de France in 1970, he was already in the viewfinder of Eddy Merckx. At the finish of that Tour, the Belgian champion—aloof, his gaze distant, lovingly sitting over his bike—answered the twenty questions he was asked all at once. He said, "Yes, I noticed a few little things.... In particular, Ocaña's great potential.... Among the French? One young rider showed himself: Bernard Thévenet, who scored a great win on the St. Gaudens–La Mongie stage." Thévenet had to wait five years to challenge Merckx. But already his victory was in the making, for, at the end of the 1974 season, this road-racer from Paray-le-Monial had come close to winning the world championship in Montréal. He was on a solo break on the last lap when he was caught by Eddy Merckx (who took the title), Frenchmen Raymond Poulidor and Mariano Martinez, and the Italian Giacinto Santambrogio. Thévenet came in fifth. Further proof that this young Frenchman was ready to claim his spot on the palmarès of the Tour came one month before the start of the 1975 race, when he won the Dauphiné Libéré, dominating Merckx and Luis Ocaña after a hard-fought struggle. He had reached full physical maturity.

That year Merckx launched the Tour at a diabolic speed toward the west, and he took over the leadership on the sixth day. For Thévenet, it was time to be on the alert. The day before tackling the Pyrenees, there was a 37-kilometer time trial, and although Merckx won again, Thévenet placed second, just nine seconds behind. In the Pyrenees he pulled back about a minute on the climb to Pla d'Adet; then he retrieved another half minute on the Puy de Dôme—where Merckx was punched in the kidneys by a spectator. So the two men were separated by just 58 seconds

when they began the next stage, the first one in the Alps. Thévenet felt that he still had a lot to offer and knew he had to attack the Belgian champion, no matter the cost. Nice to Pra-Loup promised to be the most stunning stage of the Tour. And perhaps the most heartrending....

After many attacks by Thévenet in the early part of the stage, especially on the ascent of the Col des Champs, Merckx suddenly counterattacked over the top of the Col d'Allos. Millions of television viewers had the privilege of watching the world champion's masterful plunge into the valley. The *maillot jaune* took so many risks that the press cars had to pull over precariously to give him room to pass. But suddenly, when he began the last and very tough ascent toward Pra-Loup, Merckx seemed stuck to the road. Thévenet, on the other hand, encouraged by his teammate Raymond Delisle, regained all his strength and ambition. Felice Gimondi was the first to catch and pass Merckx, and the Italian looked likely to take the victory, But, almost two minutes behind, Thévenet had taken off alone. He caught up to Lucien Van Impe, then Joop Zoetemelk. Suddenly he caught sight of Merckx on one of the hairpin turns. When Thévenet reached him, Merckx lowered his head. A fine page of Tour history was being written. The Frenchman drew alongside the Belgian, then passed him without a glance, encouraged by his Peugeot team *directeur sportif*, Maurice De Muer, who screamed, "Go, Bernard, he's had it; he's cooked!" With his momentum, Thévenet soon passed Gimondi and continued on to win the stage and take the yellow jersey. The next day, on a stage that crossed the Vars and Izoard Passes, he solidified his position, adding two minutes to his lead. Merckx was beaten. Thévenet's consecration took place on the Champs-Élysées, where the Tour finished that year for the first time. A regal road, fitting the scale of both the event and the winner. After missing the following year's race, Thévenet reappeared at the start of the 1977 Tour in Fleurance, in top form and good health. He was installed as the logical favorite, despite the presence of Merckx, Van Impe, and Zoetemelk. After nineteen days of racing, Thévenet, the *maillot jaune*, and the Dutchman Hennie Kuiper were separated by only eight seconds. The time-trial stage of 50 kilometers on the Dijon-Prenois circuit would decide the outcome. Thévenet made a more prudent start than the Dutchman, but after 15 kilometers the two were on equal footing. The Frenchman then accelerated and won the stage, beating Kuiper by 28 seconds. Thévenet had won the Tour for a second time.

Thévenet on the climb to Pra-Loup (above), the day Merckx was "laid to rest."

BERNARD THÉVENET

Born: January 10, 1948, in St. Julien-de-Civry, France
Palmarès: Tour de France 1975 and 1977. Dauphiné Libéré 1975 and 1976. Tour de Romandie 1972. Critérium National 1974. French Championship 1973.

Lucien
Van Impe
Mr. Polka Dot

Lucien Van Impe, from Mere, a small village in eastern Flanders, competed in his first Tour de France in 1969. It would be seven years before he won the event. It might have happened sooner, but Van Impe's arrival at the Tour coincided with that of another talented Belgian racer, a certain Eddy Merckx. One might suspect that Merckx's absolute reign over the plains and mountains of France gave Van Impe a number of complexes. We should add that the dapper little Belgian had long limited his ambitions at the Tour to winning the King of the Mountains, a title he would eventually claim six times, equaling the record of Federico Bahamontes. Supple and light at five feet six inches and 125 pounds, Van Impe was at ease racing at high altitudes, and, provided he was left alone to take points for the climber's classification, it was said that he was ready to sell his services to other team leaders.

A first turning point in Van Impe's Tour career came in 1975. In the hilly 40-kilometer time-trial stage between Morzine and Châtel, he defeated Merckx by a minute and realized that he, too, might be capable of

taking a Tour victory. To achieve that dream, he would need a mentor who could guide him through all the pitfalls. Then Cyrille Guimard, who had just retired from racing, was chosen as the new *directeur sportif* of Van Impe's Gitane team. An authoritarian, ambitious, imaginative, and enterprising tactician, Guimard gave the brave Lucien a tough training regimen, which put him in great shape for the start of the 1976 Tour.

Though Freddy Maertens was the early star, holding the yellow jersey for the first eight days, Van Impe was happy to await the mountains. His first goal was the ninth stage, from Divonne-les-Bains to l'Alpe d'Huez. On the final climb he found the Dutchman Joop Zoetemelk glued to his wheel. Zoetemelk won the stage, squeezing out Van Impe by three seconds. The next day brought a new victory for the Dutchman, on the summit of Montgenèvre, but as they left the Alps Van Impe wore the leader's jersey, with a 6-second lead over Zoetemelk and 1:36 over the opinionated and sturdy Raymond Poulidor. In the Pyrenees another Frenchman, Raymond Delisle, took the stage to Pyrenees 2000 by 5 minutes and grabbed the yellow jersey from Van Impe, who was now almost 3 minutes behind. The Belgian would have to attack on the fourteenth stage, St. Gaudens to St. Lary–Soulan, if he were to retake the lead. Delisle's dream quickly dissolved when Van Impe, following Guimard's orders, launched a brilliant offensive on the slopes of the Portillon Pass, a long way from the finish. Zoetemelk was also caught out and steadily lost time to the Belgian over the Peyresourde and on the steep finishing climb to Pla-d'Adet, above St. Lary. Van Impe's (and Guimard's) gamble paid off, and runner-up Zoetemelk arrived more than three minutes behind. Van Impe was finally the winner.

Van Impe was named the Tour de France King of the Mountains on six occasions, equaling the record of Bahamontes.

LUCIEN VAN IMPE

Born: October 20, 1946, in Mere, Belgium
Palmarès: Tour de France 1976, second in 1981. Tour de l'Aude 1975. Polymultipliée 1976. Best climber of Tour de France 1971, 1972, 1975, 1977, 1981, and 1983. Belgian Championship 1983.

Richard
Virenque
In the Eye of the Hurricane

To evoke the name of Virenque is—sadly—to bring back the painful memory of the Festina Affair and its dire effects on a sport undermined by doping. Until the scandals of the 1998 Tour de France everything had seemed simple for Richard Virenque. All of France had adopted this young rider from the south, creating a rising tide of Virenquemania. He was, and still is, a racer generous in his efforts, capable of beginning an attack in the first kilometers of a mountain stage and possessing the endurance to cross several passes in succession at an impressively constant speed. That was how he propelled himself to winning the polka-dot jersey of the Tour de France—symbol of the best climber—five times, just one win behind the record-holders, Bahamontes and Van Impe.

In 1992 Virenque was selected to compete at the Tour de France for the first time. After beginning at San Sebastian in northern Spain, the second stage took the race through the Pyrenees to Pau—sensational! After a marathon break through the mountains with the Spanish rider Javier Murguialdy, Virenque pulled on the yellow jersey. He had yet to achieve the least bit of success as a professional, and there he was wearing the *maillot jaune!* Virenque passed it on to his teammate Pascal Lino the next day, and his feat would not be repeated, but after that day he told the crowds that he planned on earning another distinctive jersey: the polka-dot one of best climber. In 1994, and for several years afterward, the Frenchman remained the immovable King of the Mountains at the Tour. Never was the polka-dot jersey worn with such love, and never had it been showered with such praise and warmth by the public. He realized this and said, "Each summer I live a crazy dream." How can we forget, then, his epic rides to Luz-Ardiden in 1994, Cauterets in 1995, Courchevel (with Ullrich) in 1997, and Morzine in 2000? But sometimes dreams come crashing down. Technological advances, the progress of science, and the demands of life sometimes lead us to cross the threshold between the acceptable and the inexcusable. International cycling was hit head-on by the 1998 doping scandal, and it is still struggling to recover. On July 8, 1998, the Festina Affair exploded when the trainer Willy Voet was arrested in the north of France, on his way from his Belgian home to the Tour start in Dublin. Customs officers uncovered a cargo of doping substances in his Festina team vehicle—in total almost four hundred flasks, many of which were confirmed to contain the banned drug EPO. Almost every member of Virenque's Festina team confessed to using this type of product. All nine of its Tour riders were dismissed from the race at the dawn of the seventh stage.

Virenque cried over his broken dreams and his shattered illusions. But another drama was unfolding. The prestigious climber had not admitted to having taken part, with his comrades, in the EPO injections. Unlike his teammates, he therefore did not receive an eight-month suspension. But justice was not going to let him go. While he signed a profitable contract with the Italian team, Polti, and while he won a stage of the Giro d'Italia and took back his King of the Mountains title at the Tour de France, he knew that one day he would have to spit on his own destiny in a court-room. That day arrived at the end of the year 2000, and the demigod of the mountains tumbled down to the level of a common criminal.

Virenque forever remains the idol of the crowds despite his confessions, as painful as they were late.

RICHARD VIRENQUE

Born: November 19, 1969, in Casablanca, Morocco
Palmarès: Paris-Tours 2001. Tour of Piedmont 1996. Climber's Trophy 1994. Grand Prix de la Marseillaise 1997. Best climber of Tour de France in 1994, 1995, 1996, 1997, and 1999.

Joop Zoetemelk
The Complete Work

Joop Zoetemelk didn't win the Tour de France until his tenth attempt, in 1980. For a whole decade the Dutchman's path to the top of the podium was barred by one racer or another—specifically Eddy Merckx, Bernard Hinault, Luis Ocaña, and Lucien Van Impe. It was frustrating for Zoetemelk because since his Tour debut in 1970 he had always figured in the places of honor: five times in second place, twice in fourth, and once in fifth! And when in 1974 he seemed to have the beating of Merckx after winning Paris-Nice, the Setmana Catalana, and the Tour de Romandie, a horrific accident at the Midi Libre kept him out of the Tour. It took the Dutchman several years to put the aftereffects of that crash completely behind him. But his courage and perseverance allowed him to regain his place in the peloton. Then the dominant Bernard Hinault arrived on the scene, and it seemed that Zoetemelk would be deprived of any future possibility of victory. But it would take something more than that to unsettle the Dutch racer—who since his marriage had lived just outside Paris in Germigny-l'Évêque—who went in search of other laurels, all the while conducting his career with perfect honesty.

Zoetemelk understood that in order to win the Tour, he needed to be supported by the finest possible team. So in 1980 he joined the Dutch team, TI Raleigh, which was directed by a sort of sorcerer by the name of Peter Post. Zoetemelk now had a team as strong as Hinault's Renault squad. As it happened, tendinitis of the knee forced Hinault to quit the race after twelve days, when he was leading the Tour by just 21 seconds over Zoetemelk. The way was finally open for the Dutchman, and we can be sure that the good Joop had every right to his eventual victory that year. Before winning the Tour, Zoetemelk had proved to be a champion in many other arenas. As an amateur he won an Olympic gold medal in the team time trial at Mexico in 1968 and followed this triumph with an impressive victory in the Tour de l'Avenir, already showing the skills of an experienced veteran. He should have used this experience to his advantage. But Merckx was already dominating the pro scene by then, and Joop had to submit to the Belgian's hegemony. Tragedy was near. On May 22, 1974, at the Midi Libre stage race, as the peloton was coming into a stage finish at the beach town of Valras-Plage, an illegally parked car caused twelve racers to fall. The most seriously injured was Zoetemelk. There was talk of a fractured skull. It was an apparently dying man who was transported to the Suresnes hospital in Paris. Cycling disappeared from his horizon. His bad luck did not get the better of him, though he returned too soon to the peloton. The treatment he had just undergone had decreased the number of red blood cells in his body. He lost his sense of smell, a sign of meningitis, and he was reportedly afflicted with a medulla hypoplasia. The least effort made him suffer. One man figured it out: Dr. Fucs, a medical practitioner from Nice who had a knack for solving difficult cases. Even after being healed, Zoetemelk was no longer quite the same. But he embarked on a second career that took him to the highest levels. To his Tour success he added a win at the Vuelta a España and three Paris-Nice victories. In single-day races, he won the Flèche Wallonne and two editions of Paris-Tours. At age thirty-eight he became the world road champion at Montello, Italy, and capped his career two years later by winning the Dutch classic, the Amstel Gold Race, at age forty. It was an opus wisely accomplished. The unassuming charm of a *maillot jaune*.

After being subjected to the reign of Eddy Merckx, Zoetemelk then saw Hinault burst onto the scene. He did not give up.

JOOP ZOETEMELK

Born: December 3, 1946, in The Hague, the Netherlands
Palmarès: World Championship 1985. Tour de France 1980 (second a record six times). Vuelta a España 1979. Paris-Nice 1974, 1975, and 1979. Tour de Romandie 1974. Tirreno-Adriatico 1985. Setmana Catalana 1974. Tour de l'Avenir 1969. Amstel Gold Race 1987. Flèche Wallonne 1976. Paris-Tours 1977 (Tours-Versailles) and 1979 (Blois-Chaville). Olympic Gold Medal in the 100-km Team Time Trial 1968.

THE CLASSICS

Olivier Dazat, a passionate writer on cycling, contends that there is a breed of racer "considered, much like those famous batteries, to last a little longer than the others." In this final chapter we have grouped together those who have always held the secret of the "classics"—those who, throughout their entire careers, in all types of weather, throughout the year, have evolved in a school of suffering, able to withstand any kind of hardship. From the start to the end of the season, they rivaled each other in vigor, vitality, and nervous energy. The classics, as we have baptized them, have never spared the body—they burn up all its resources while the heart is at the point of explosion. Many Flemish riders, called *flahutes* in French, are in this category—those very riders who find their paradise in the "hell of the North." Sometimes matching the Belgians are Italians—including men such as the excellent Michele Bartoli—and some Frenchmen, starting with Laurent Fignon, whose credentials were so strong that he could have been featured in every chapter of this book.

Vittorio
Adorni
Stamina and Style

In Italy they said he forced his nature to change from a gentleman-cyclist into a nobleman-cyclist. At the start of the 1960s there was little use for a handkerchief in the peloton, and you had to be called Hugo Koblet to get away with pulling out a comb before facing the crowds and the photographers, not to mention the television cameras. But Vittorio Adorni, a citizen of Parma and a former worker at the Barilla pasta company, devoted himself to becoming such a gentleman-nobleman.

When he first tried out cycling, his uncle encouraged him to persevere. He certainly had a natural elegance, and his "look" on the bike was inspirational. On his own machine, though, he was reluctant to use any excessive effort—at least that was the impression he gave.

By 1963 it was evident that he had a fine career ahead of him when he finished second at the Giro d'Italia. He was still on the lookout for a big success, though, and he thought he might find it at the 1964 world championship on the tough circuit at Sallanches, France. On the final lap Adorni broke away with Jan Janssen and Raymond Poulidor, putting much of his energy into the attack. Unfortunately, he could do nothing against Janssen's final sprint. Second at the Giro, second at the world's, he promised himself that one day he would win both these races.

It took Adorni two years to achieve his first goal. In 1965 he won the Giro—and was discovered by television. He spoke a very distinguished Italian, and through his influence cycling penetrated into the most upper-crust circles. He shattered the image of cycling as a sport for old troopers. He received constant invitations to talk about his races on television. Let's not pretend that he whistled *Aïda* as he rode, and that in the evenings, while the others dreamed only of victory, he was thinking about box seats at the Regio di Parma opera house.

But Adorni's racing career was yet to be accomplished. He crowned that career at age thirty-one by winning the world championship on the Imola circuit, not far from his home. That year, 1968, had been a difficult one for him because he, a proud Italian, rode for a Belgian, Eddy Merckx. Even though

their team was sponsored by Faema, an Italian manufacturer of coffee machines, Adorni was accused of being a "merckxenary."

In that 1968 race for the rainbow jersey Adorni was present from the outset in a breakaway that also included Rik Van Looy of Belgium. They stayed together for three hours, taking an enormous 10-minute lead. Then, with 93 kilometers still to ride, Adorni confirmed his role as the strongman in the breakaway group: He attacked, dropped Van Looy and the others, and rode solo all the way to the finish. He had won his world championship in splendid fashion, as he did some fifty other races in his career. Maybe he could have won more, but he was always concerned with the quality and style of his successes.

On his retirement from racing, Adorni returned to television, this time as the anchor of a show completely unrelated to cycling, proving that he was a man of many talents. He radiated sympathy, courtesy, tact, intelligence, and diplomacy. It was said again that he was too handsome to suffer. In truth, he suffered a great deal, and once an ordeal was over he would relate his experiences in a clear voice that rejected easy heroism.

VITTORIO ADORNI

Born: November 14, 1937, in San Lazzaro di Parma, Italy

Palmarès: World Championship 1968. Italian Championship 1969. Giro d'Italia 1965. Tour of Belgium 1966. Tour of Switzerland 1969. Tour de Romandie 1965 and 1967. Tour of Sardinia 1964. Grand Prix of Lugano 1966.

Vittorio Adorni, the gentleman-cyclist, finished his career with a world champion's jersey.

went so hard that only the Frenchman Charly Mottet was able to stick to his wheel. This lead was still not enough for the Venetian. With 5 kilometers to go, on a short climb, he attacked with all his strength. Mottet faltered but just managed to catch back up on a descent before the uphill finish. However, Argentin knew he had a better sprint than the Frenchman and saw that Mottet looked worn out from his brutal attacks. The result: Moreno Argentin, the great hope of the Italians, was only their second world road champion in thirteen years.

Moreno
Argentin
Prince of the Ardennes

By finishing third in the 1985 world road championship in Italy, then winning the title in 1986 in the United States before placing second in 1987 in Austria, Moreno Argentin pulled off a series that would go down in history. He was, after all, only the third racer of all time to stand on each of the three steps of the podium at the world's, following in the footsteps of the Dutchman Theo Middelkamp and the Frenchman André Darrigade.

Born in December 1960 to a family of farm workers, Argentin began his cycling career on the velodromes of his native Veneto region. After forty-one victories as an amateur, he turned pro in 1980 and made his name by winning, almost every year, one or more stages at the Giro d'Italia. But he wanted international recognition. This wish was finally granted in 1985, when he won Belgium's superclassic Liège-Bastogne-Liège. He would win that hilly race in the Ardennes three more times. Then, after his third place at the 1985 world's behind Joop Zoetemelk and Greg LeMond, he won the supreme title at Colorado Springs in 1986.

It was cold that day on the Air Force Academy circuit, the sun hidden by low clouds hanging over the Rockies. At the front, Argentin, who had launched the decisive breakaway and worked hard for its success, felt that he needed to accelerate again to split up the group. Sure of himself, he

Argentin was representative of a new Italy—vibrant and brash, courageous to the point of recklessness—that, beyond cycling, was asserting itself in the realms of fashion, technology, and entrepreneurship. In light of Argentin's results in the single-day classics, he is indisputably worthy of figuring in the company of the sport's giants—with his victories in Liège-Bastogne-Liège, the Flèche Wallonne, Tour of Flanders, Tour of Lombardy, and the world championship. He was called the Fleming with an Italian flavor.

His finishing sprints were measured by their quality rather than their quantity. He was no mountain climber, but he was powerful on short climbs, and though he was uncomfortable on the flats, this shrewd tactician knew how, in one judicious maneuver, to give his all at just the right moment.

Argentin, the Italian racer who was more Flemish than the Flemish, was crowned world champion at Colorado Springs in 1986 (above).

MORENO ARGENTIN

Born: December 17, 1960, in San Dona di Piave, Italy
Palmarès: World Championship 1986. Italian Championship 1983 and 1989. Liège-Bastogne-Liège 1985, 1986, 1987, and 1991. Flèche Wallonne 1990, 1991, and 1994. Tour of Flanders 1990. Tour of Lombardy 1987. Tour of Sicily 1984. Tour of Denmark 1985. Giro del Trentino 1994.

Ercole
Baldini
The Hercules of Forli

Ercole Baldini had all the qualities of a true *campionissimo,* yet his role in the evolution of Italian cycling leaves the impression of unfinished work. He might have made a few mistakes, in part because he had fragile health and a tendency to give up when the going got tough.

His cycling career began in 1951. Then, as a completely unknown twenty-one-year-old at the October 1954 week of records organized at the Vigorelli velodrome in Milan, he covered 44.870 kilometers in an hour record attempt, to break the world amateur mark. Two years later, when he was still in the amateur ranks, he did even better, breaking the outright world hour record of Jacques Anquetil with a distance of 46.393 kilometers. Also before turning professional Baldini won the world amateur pursuit title in Copenhagen and claimed the Olympic road race gold medal in Melbourne.

Baldini began his professional career in 1957 like an express train, placing third in the Giro d'Italia, winning the Italian road championship, and then

taking the Baracchi Trophy with Fausto Coppi. But it was the following year that Baldini secured his place in cycling history. At the Giro he annihilated the opposition in the time trials and clinched the overall victory with a long solo break to Verona. Later in the year, a few days before the world road championship, he defeated Aldo Moser to win the semiclassic Matteoti Trophy, positioning himself among the favorites for the world's. The starting lineup on the day of the world championship, on the Reims automobile circuit in the Champagne region of France, was simply breathtaking: Anquetil, Coppi, Louison Bobet, Rik Van Looy, Rik Van Steenbergen, André Darrigade…. Four men found themselves in command well before half the distance had been covered: Bobet, Gastone Nencini, Gerrit Voorting, and … Baldini. On the eleventh climb of the Prémecy hill, the Dutchman Voorting dropped back; the Italian Nencini, feeling his strength abandoning him, approached his compatriot, Baldini, and secretly urged him, "Go on, attack. Take off alone!" So Baldini accelerated the next time up the Prémecy climb. Nencini fell back, as anticipated … and Bobet too, meter by meter. There were 50 kilometers left. The Italian covered them solo, to finish two minutes ahead of the runner-up, Bobet. A perfect triumph.

It seemed that Italy had discovered its successor to Bartali, Coppi, Magni…. But it was only an illusion. In this event, the soft, peaceful, melancholy Ercole had experienced a culmination rather than a grand entrance. One sensed in him a difficulty in surpassing himself—a lack of the sort of self-transcendence that usually sanctifies a supremely endowed champion, a superstar in the eyes of the crowds. Friendship provided him with an outlet for his natural generosity. He surprised all those who had decided he was an austere athlete. He subdued the colorful Raphaël Geminiani by gulping down more ice cream cones in one week than the average person could consume in a year.

Baldini's position on the bicycle was near perfection. He was completely in harmony with his machine, a model of style and quiet power. After his crushing success at the world championship in 1958, his decline was slow but inevitable. At times some breaks in the clouds appeared, but the general outlook remained gray. At the end of 1964 Baldini put away his bike for good, but he never lost his natural kindness and compassion.

ERCOLE BALDINI

Born: January 26, 1933, in Villanova di Forli, Italy
Palmarès: World Championship 1958. Italian Championship 1957. Giro d'Italia 1958. Grand Prix des Nations 1960. Baracchi Trophy 1957 (with Fausto Coppi), 1958 and 1959 (both with Aldo Moser), and 1961 (with Jo Velly). Olympic Road Race Gold Medal 1956. World Hour Record 1956 (46.393 km).

With more tenacity, Baldini might have joined the Italian legends Coppi, Bartali, and Magni.

Michele
Bartoli
Well-Earned Classics

There is a breed of Italian racer that loves to race the events of northern Europe and win the classics that adorn the international calendar. One who performed well in the rain of Belgium was Fiorenzo Magni; another, more recently, was Moreno Argentin. Now there is another specimen, Michele Bartoli, who won consecutive editions of Liège-Bastogne-Liège and the UCI World Cup in 1997–1998.

Turning pro in 1992, he signed a contract with the Mercatone Uno team. Soon after the legendary *directeur sportif* Giancarlo Ferretti, who had yet to invite him to join his team, expressed an interest in the newcomer. He said that Bartoli was the most promising rider in a brilliant new generation of Italian racers—that of Pantani, Casagrande, Rebellin. ... Ferretti proved persuasive, and in 1996 the Tuscan came under his control.

Bartoli soon acquired a taste for Belgian races, conducting himself like a veteran in the cool, humid conditions of Flanders, learning how to combat the wind and even use it to his advantage. His talent quickly developed, and Ferretti guided him to a brilliant solo victory in the Tour of Flanders.

Twelve months later, on April 20, 1997, Bartoli reached a state of grace at Liège-Bastogne-Liège, where he completed one of the finest exploits of the year. Nearing the finish at Ans, in the outskirts of Liège, were just three riders with a shot at winning this classic: Laurent Jalabert, Alex Zülle, and Bartoli. The latter looked by far the strongest and knew he could get away from his opponents when he was ready. Zülle was the first one who dropped. Soon afterward Bartoli stood on his pedals and decided to make a long, full-blown sprint. It was over for Jalabert, the winner of the Flèche Wallonne four days earlier. For Bartoli it was a well-earned consecration. He followed that win with solid performances at the year's other great classics to clinch overall victory in the UCI World Cup.

Now let's move to 1998, year two of his supremacy. The early season events reinforced his goals. Henceforth it was best for Bartoli to think like a Fleming in order to prepare for the Belgian races. He liked this genre of event: selective, played out in difficult climatic conditions. The result: sixth place at the Tour of Flanders, fifth at the Flèche Wallonne. But though he was placing well, he was lacking the slight edge needed for supreme success. This came, once again, at Liège-Bastogne-Liège. Bartoli carried out his first attack on La Redoute, the severe climb about 35 kilometers from the finish, and repeated the move with 15 kilometers to go, to end the race alone, more than one minute ahead of Jalabert. This victory put Bartali at the head of the World Cup, and he stayed there for the rest of the season, picking up a second World Cup event, the Grand Prix of Zurich, in a furious sprint against Frank Vandenbroucke.

Bartoli has character. Without seeing him contort himself on his machine, it is impossible to understand how relentlessly he assaults his body. He extracts every last ounce of energy from himself. He flies like the wind on insane gear ratios. He has breeding and a fierce passion. In Italy that is called *rabbia*—a rage to win.

Bartoli, winner of the 1996 Tour of Flanders (left), is one of today's top classics riders—a pure talent.

MICHELE BARTOLI

Born: May 27, 1970, in Pisa, Italy
Palmarès: Liège-Bastogne-Liège 1997 and 1998. Tour of Flanders 1996. Amstel Gold Race 2002. Grand Prix of Frankfurt 1997. Championship of Zürich 1998. Flèche Wallonne 1999. Grand Prix of Plouay 2000. Italian Championship 2000. Het Volk 2001. Tour of Sicily 1993. Three Days of De Panne 1995 and 1998. Tirreno-Adriatico 1999. Mediterranean Tour 2002. UCI World Cup 1997 and 1998.

Chris
Boardman
The Fastest in the World

He spent all of his athletic life playing with numbers. It all started in 1993, on the wooden track of the Bordeaux-Lac stadium, where Chris Boardman improved the world hour record to 52.270 kilometers. Then, on September 6, 1996, the Briton showed an even more mind-blowing performance by covering 56.375 kilometers in the hour in front of his own fans at the velodrome in Manchester. Using his extended handlebars in the so-called Superman position, he shattered the world record held by the Swiss Tony Rominger. He also broke the world record in the 4,000-meter individual pursuit with a time of 4:11.114.

Boardman's first coup dates back to the 1992 Olympics in Barcelona. Riding a revolutionary superbike built by Lotus, he took the gold medal in the pursuit back to his modest brick house on Walker Street in Hoylake, the old fishing village on the Irish Sea where he was born, now the industrial gateway to Liverpool.

Boardman launched his career as a road racer in September 1993 after being invited to join the French team, Gan, by its *directeur sportif* Roger Legeay. Yet again he let his speed speak for him by winning three Tour de France prologues—at Lille (1994), Rouen (1997), and Dublin (1998). At Lille he completed his prologue at an average speed of 55.152 kilometers per hour over the 7.2-kilometer course—the fastest circuit time trial in history. In fact, his victorious prologues remain the three fastest on a circuit. But though these victories—earning him the *maillot jaune* each time—

were statements of his success, the prologue at the 1995 Tour remains imprinted in his mind. On a dark evening at St. Brieuc in Brittany, he set off under a battering rain on a circuit that began with a narrow descent of sharp curves, which made it hard to see what was ahead. Boardman raced down this slalom with extreme motivation, but the adrenaline high made him reckless. On a sweeping turn his back tire skidded and he slid out of control, striking a crash barrier. The outcome: multiple fractures of the ankle.

Three years later, after taking his third Tour prologue win on O'Connell Street, Dublin, before fervent Irish crowds, Boardman played out another drama. While still leading the race on the second stage as the fast-moving peloton entered County Cork, Boardman collided with the rear wheel of his teammate Frédéric Moncassin. The blood-stained *maillot jaune* stayed down. Once more his Tour was cut short. Boardman had set the age of his athletic retirement at thirty-two. However, it was at that moment that the sport's governing body, the UCI, decided to place an enormous check on technological progress. It announced that future attempts at the world hour record would have as a target the distance of 49.431 kilometers covered by Eddy Merckx in 1972—requiring a traditional bike and components comparable to those used by the great Belgian. To crown his career, Chris Boardman decided to accept the challenge.

At the end of October 2000 the Briton entered the track in Manchester before a capacity crowd. There was an electric pulse of expectancy. Would he be able to go faster than Merckx? Boardman started off more slowly than Merckx had. His progress was wrapped in suspense, and after an almost inhuman effort in the final laps, he finished with 49.441 kilometers—just 10 meters ahead of the symbolic record designated by the UCI. He'd succeeded by little more than one turn of the pedals. An unprecedented determination had carried Boardman to his ultimate hour of glory. He had returned a human dimension to the world hour record.

CHRIS BOARDMAN

Born: August 28, 1968 in Hoylake, England
Palmarès: World Time Trial Champion 1994. Grand Prix des Nations 1996. Critérium International 1996. Grand Prix Eddy Merckx 1993 and 1996. Olympic Pursuit Gold Medal 1992. World Pursuit Championship 1994 and 1996. Tour de France prologue 1994, 1997, and 1998. World Hour Record 1993 (52.270 km) and 1996 (56.375 km). World Hour Record (new standard) 2000 (49.441 km).

Boardman spent most of his career pushing limits in order to set record times.

Gianni
Bugno
Listening to Mozart

Out of the amateur ranks a champion in the making had emerged, a rider of multiple strengths whose great class matched his capabilities. His name was Gianni Bugno, and he first proved his abilities as a time trialist at the core of the Italian national team in the 100-kilometer team time trial; as a climber when he won Monaco-Alassio; and as a sprinter when he won, on two occasions, the Italian amateur championship on points. He knew what it meant to work hard and, even more so, that success came only at the expense of great effort.

Born in Brugg, Switzerland, in 1964, he was the son of an Italian immigrant worker, a carpenter named Giacomo. The family moved to Venice, where an interesting job had taken his father, but Gianni grew up mostly in Monza, near Milan. After four years of study he left technical school, and the world of cycling beckoned. Bugno claims to have been drawn to cycling at a young age, enthralled by the various passages of the Giro d'Italia and the Tour of Lombardy through his hometown. Before long the local club, Ciclisti Monzesi, managed by Nazzareno Cazzaniga,

saw a new member turn up, full of ambition. Bugno's amateur performances eventually drew the attention of professional teams, and in particular the *directeur sportif* of Atala, ex–road racer Franco Cribiori. So in September 1985 Bugno turned pro for Atala and soon became the great hope of Italian cycling when he defeated Francesco Moser in a sprint to win the Tour of the Apennines. Too soon he was given the role of team leader. That responsibility was hard for him to bear, especially as he demanded nothing more than to learn his trade well. But in the late 1980s the Italian public demanded stars. Bugno did not fully believe in his abilities, and his development was delayed.

In 1988 he moved to the bigger Château d'Ax team, took a stage of the Tour de France at Limoges, and won half a dozen important races in Italy. It was not enough, though. An accident at that year's Giro almost ruined everything. The unsuspected consequence: a damaged eardrum. That injury explained why he became a mediocre descender, overcome by fear. This problem reached an extreme at October's Milan-Turin race. Bugno had reached the summit of a small pass in the front of the race, accompanied by the German Rolf Gölz—but before reaching the valley he was overtaken by three separate groups. The vertigo was stronger than his willpower. Bugno's entourage decided to consult a specialist, a Frenchwoman by the name of Laura Bertelé who practiced at a hospital in Milan. For a month, Bugno followed a treatment there, based on ultrasound, that was intended to repair his atrophied eardrum. The treatment also required him to listen regularly to pieces of classical music—in his case, Mozart. The cure was beneficial. Soon the downhills no longer terrified him. His victory in the 1990 Milan–San Remo proved that.

From that time forward, if he experienced any dizziness, it was that of success. With his complexes behind him Bugno became a true leader, winning the Giro d'Italia that same year—capturing the pink jersey on the first day and keeping it until the end. In all types of races he proved his dominance. The following year he placed second behind Miguel Indurain at the Tour de France—in which he outsped the Spaniard to win the prestigious Alpe d'Huez stage. Bugno went on to win the world championship at Stuttgart, a feat he repeated in 1992 at Benidorm, where he finished ahead of Laurent Jalabert. Altogether, Gianni Bugno's career stretched across thirteen years and eighty victories.

Though he was good on all terrain,
Bugno lacked a little something to become a campionissimo.

GIANNI BUGNO

Born: February 16, 1964, in Brugg, Switzerland
Palmarès: World Championship 1991 and 1992. Italian Championship 1991 and 1995. Giro d'Italia 1990. Tour of Flanders 1994. Milan–San Remo 1990. Clasica San Sebastian 1991. Wincanton Classic 1990. Giro del Lazio 1994. Tour of Piedmont 1986. Milan-Turin 1992. Giro del Trentino 1990. Mediterranean Tour 1995. Second in Tour de France 1991. UCI World Cup 1990.

Roger
De Vlaeminck
The Story of the Gypsy

Little by little Roger De Vlaeminck gained respect with his dramatic, repeated feats in Paris-Roubaix, which led to four victories, and with his splendidly successful week in October 1976, when he scored three classic wins in six days: the Tour of Emilia, the Agostoni Cup, and the Tour of Lombardy. With this latter coup, he snubbed his national cycling federation, which had left him off its team for the world championships in Ostuni. The federation's decision may have been an act of revenge by its officials, who had not forgiven De Vlaeminck for refusing to defend his world cyclo-cross title six months earlier. It was through cyclo-cross that this sullen Flemish rider, with his supple, elegant silhouette, had acquired the demon-like agility that made him as comfortable on the slippery cobblestones of Paris-Roubaix as he was in

mass sprint finishes, battling against Freddy Maertens one-on-one. The two men were steadfast rivals.

They called him "the Gypsy" because his father had married a "gypsy" woman. Not that Laura De Vlaeminck, née Six, was ethnically a Romany, but she belonged to those traveling peoples, roving merchants, who moved through Flanders in colorfully painted wagons, selling their wares.... They settled in Eeklo—the husband's hometown—where the little De Vlaemincks, Eric, Roger, and their little sister, grew up in a modest cottage at the edge of town between wealthy-looking farms and neatly aligned hop fields. After devoting much of his teenaged years to soccer, Roger decided to try cycling. A friend whose parents owned a bike shop lent him a machine, and as soon as he began racing in 1964 he accumulated an impressive number of victories.

He had already won a world title—the amateurs' cyclo-cross championship—before he turned pro in 1969 with a huge ambition. And by winning the semiclassic Het Volk and the national road championship, he went straight into the inner circle of Belgian pros. From there began his rivalry with Eddy Merckx, marked by his 1970 victory at Liège-Bastogne-Liège. Soon came his first win at Paris-Roubaix (1972), a race he not only won four times but also finished four times in second place. He spent most of his career with Italian teams, often competing in Italy, where he won a first victory at Tirreno-Adriatico in 1972, followed by five others in that spring stage race along with stage wins at the Giro d'Italia, three Milan–San Remo victories, and two Tours of Lombardy. He was then struck by a great misfortune: his brother's confinement in a psychiatric hospital for drug use. Roger kept going to inspire his brother, who had until that time dominated cyclo-cross with seven world titles. Roger pitted his strength against Merckx, defeated him in Milan–San Remo, and accompanied him in a breakaway on a mountain stage of the Giro. He approved of Merckx and, somewhere inside, admired him. And he was proud of what former Belgian great Rik Van Looy wrote in a popular Flemish newspaper on January 2, 1973: "Roger De Vlaeminck is the most gifted and the only genuine racer of classics in his generation."

The Tour of Lombardy was the ideal expression for De Vlaeminck. He won it in 1976, ahead of Thévenet and Panizza.

ROGER DE VLAEMINCK

Born: August 24, 1947, in Eeklo, Belgium
Palmarès: Belgian Championship 1969 and 1981. Liège-Bastogne-Liège 1970. Paris-Roubaix 1972, 1974, 1975, and 1977. Milan–San Remo 1973, 1978, and 1979. Tour of Lombardy 1974 and 1976. Tour of Flanders 1977. Championship of Zürich 1975. Flèche Wallonne 1971. Giro del Lazio 1975 and 1976. Paris-Brussels 1981. Milan-Turin 1972 and 1974. Tour of Piedmont 1977. Het Volk 1969 and 1979. Tour of Switzerland 1975. Tirreno-Adriatico 1972, 1973, 1974, 1975, 1976, and 1977. Four Days of Dunkirk 1971. Tour of Sicily 1974. World Cyclo-Cross Championship 1975.

Gilbert
Duclos-Lassalle
His Paradise Was "Hell"

Gilbert Duclos-Lassalle was the fourth child in a family of small farmers from Lembeye, at the foot of the Pyrenees. He denies having been a spoiled child—sheltered, perhaps. He learned a trade; obtained a mechanic's certificate; and, after a straightforward amateur career, turned pro in 1977, becoming an integral member of the Peugeot team. He won Paris-Nice in 1980, following a long breakaway across the snow-covered hills of the Forez with fellow Frenchman Pierre Bazzo. He later won the Tour du Tarn … then competed in Paris-Roubaix. He was given just one piece of advice: Keep an eye on two-time defending champion Francesco Moser. Duclos-Lassalle did not let Moser out of his sight all day. The kilometers passed by. Soon it was just he and the Italian at the front of the race; then a fall and then a puncture shattered the Frenchman's hopes. He came in second, but he knew then that one day this "Hell of the North" would become his most beautiful paradise.

He liked the big battles. With his natural strength and power, you could see him winning a race like the marathon Bordeaux-Paris classic. After an unlucky experience in 1981 he attempted the race again in 1983, on the advice of his assistant *directeur sportif* and confidant, Roger Legeay. Duclos-Lassalle cleverly based his preparation for Bordeaux-Paris on that of the Belgian Herman Van Springel, a seven-time winner. He went to Belgium, where he raced in the kermesse circuit races and did diabolically hard training rides. The training worked, and he won Bordeaux-Paris.

More than ever, though, the desire to win Paris-Roubaix ate away at him. He had to wait until April 12, 1992, to realize his dream. That day, on the cobblestones of the North, Duclos-Lassalle rode away from his last two breakaway companions 46 kilometers from the end. Olaf Ludwig—a fine racer from the former East Germany—made a late counterattack. With 4 kilometers to go, the gap between the two was no more than 28 seconds. But "Gibus," as the journalists had christened him, still had plenty of reserves. He accelerated; the race was won. The crowd chanted his name; the enthusiasm was at a frenzy inside the velodrome at Roubaix. He crossed the line in a daze.

The following year he returned. On April 10, the day before the classic, the main headline in L'Équipe, the French sports paper, read: "Will He Do It Again?" The intriguing title had the air of a premonition. In this 1993 race, as the kilometers unfolded, it appeared that the Italian Franco Ballerini was riding the strongest. Fifty kilometers from the finish, thirteen riders were still together at the front, including Ballerini and Duclos-Lassalle. The Frenchman was watching a certain Italian, just as he had done a decade earlier with Moser: This time it was Ballerini. Thirty kilo-

meters from the end the two were the only ones left from the break. The Italian was literally flying, and the experienced Frenchman, with typical craftiness, refused to take the lead. Then they arrived in the velodrome and began a furious sprint. They crossed the line so locked together that the judges had to study the photo finish to decide the winner.

"After viewing the film, the winner is Gilbert Duclos-Lassalle," said the speaker, Daniel Mangeas, "… by 8 centimeters." The Monday edition of L'Équipe was able to answer its Saturday headline, this time writing: "He did it!"

Duclos-Lassalle won Paris-Roubaix in 1993, for the second consecutive year, just a length ahead of Ballerini (above).

GILBERT DUCLOS-LASSALLE

Born: August 25, 1954, in Lembeye, France
Palmarès: Paris-Roubaix 1992 and 1993. Paris-Nice 1980. Midi Libre 1991. Tour of Corsica 1980 and 1982. Bordeaux-Paris 1983. Tour of Sweden 1986. Grand Prix de Plouay 1981 and 1987.

Laurent
Fignon
Like a Sun

Laurent Fignon had an uneventful childhood, completed his studies, went to college, and finally made a career for himself in bike racing. Born in central Paris, he moved with his family several years later to Tournan-en-Brie, in the southeast suburbs.

In March 1982 he won his first significant victory: the Critérium International. On the second day he slipped deftly into a breakaway that developed in the hill-climbing stage while his team leader, Bernard Hinault, was held hostage by the peloton. On that day we tipped our hats to the opportunism of the young professional, who continued to work in Hinault's shadow, impatiently awaiting the day when he could be the leader himself. His day would come—and he wouldn't have to wait too long.

The following season Hinault found himself at odds with the Renault *directeur sportif* Cyrille Guimard; he also developed tendinitis and could not defend his Tour de France title. The way was open to Fignon, only twenty-two, who captured the *maillot jaune* on L'Alpe d'Huez and went on to win his first Tour de France.

In 1984, back in the peloton, Hinault had not yet regained his full power.

He had to readapt. This was his period of greatest struggle. Fignon, meanwhile, was on the rise. There he was in the Giro d'Italia, defeated by Francesco Moser only after some dubious goings-on. In the mountains Fignon had largely dominated his rival, but the Italian organizers saved Moser by eliminating the biggest climb, the Stelvio, pointing to the light snow that had fallen overnight. At Corvara, in the Dolomites, Fignon donned the pink jersey after a solo break across the Gardena and Pordoï Passes. Moser was able to limit the damage by getting the help of several allies hidden in the peloton. All that remained was a perfectly straight 42-kilometer, flat time-trial stage from Soave to Verona. The young Frenchman was ready to fight hard but had no illusions: "When I saw Moser with his special bike—like the one he used to break the world hour record—I realized that it was over," he admitted. "That machine gave him a two-seconds-a-kilometer advantage." Moser easily swallowed the 1:31 deficit he held and added a further minute to win the Giro. Fignon was adamant that without the aid of his sophisticated equipment Moser would not have beaten him.

That same year one could say there was a real Hinault-Fignon duel on the roads of the Tour de France. Hinault won the prologue, but Fignon moved in front of him in the second stage. Hinault, having undergone surgery on his leg, was still riding a notch below the form of his opponent. He battled hard, but Fignon was untouchable in the final week and easily won his second Tour.

The two men had a common trait: They both had a way of inspiring an instinctive sympathy or antipathy. They never failed to make an impression. They both had "character." Guimard, like a good teacher, had an admirable understanding of Fignon. When he went too far the *directeur sportif* was able to provide the necessary corrective measures. He also figured out how to make Fignon go faster in time trials and, not to leave anything out, how to develop extra power. According to Guimard, Fignon had held on too long to the brooding hesitations of adolescence and, on reaching adulthood, had transformed his inner aggression into an outward panache....

Fignon's victories bore the mark of his temperament—a temperament that could produce nothing but a genuine champion.

Fignon's 1984 Tour de France
was as handsome
and hot as a summer sun.

LAURENT FIGNON

Born: August 12, 1960, in Paris, France
Palmarès: Tour de France 1983 and 1984 (second in 1989). Giro d'Italia 1989 (second in 1984). Tour de l'Avenir 1988. Tour of Mexico 1993. Milan–San Remo 1988 and 1989. Critérium International 1982. Flèche Wallonne 1986. Grand Prix des Nations 1989. Baracchi Trophy 1989 (with Thierry Marie). French Championship 1984.

Jean Forestier
The Lyon Heart

A generous, pensive spirit of the highest caliber, unpretentious to the point of self-effacement, too shy and too private, Jean Forestier was missing the spark that gives greatness its splendor. He avoided confrontation, fled from interviews, and distrusted the public. Yet, what a wonderful racer!

He explained his character as the product of a temperament particular to natives of Lyon, where he was born in 1930. His father worked in the city slaughterhouses when little Jean and his brothers came into the world. These butcher's sons were not in a position to wait long before choosing their jobs. Jean had a pathological horror of blood and said he preferred work as a mechanic. He began an apprenticeship with a former racer and became a bike mechanic. In trying out the bikes, ensuring that they were working properly, he gradually became a bike racer himself. Forestier had a labored start to his career, not always finishing his races and often fading at a crucial moment. It was not until after his military service that he began to win all the races in his local area. Sponsored by a small regional bike company, Follis, he refused to leave Lyon to go to Paris—then the key to cycling glory. Selected for one of the five French regional teams at the 1953 Tour de France, he lost his chance for a breakthrough on home soil, in the Briançon-Lyon stage, when he was beaten by his Nord-Est-Centre teammate Georges Meunier. In

1954 Forestier reluctantly agreed to ride Switzerland's Tour de Romandie. After a long, crazy breakaway on the very first stage, he took the overall lead and managed to keep it for the whole race, to defeat men like Fiorenzo Magni, Hugo Koblet, and Ferdi Kubler.

This performance earned him selection to the French national team at the Tour, in which he devoted himself to helping Louison Bobet win the race. He also had the satisfaction, with the protection of his teammates, of winning in his hometown, taking the sixteenth stage, Le Puy–Lyon, in a seven-man sprint.

Forestier's career stepped up a level in 1955 when he won Paris-Roubaix. About 30 kilometers from the finish he dropped his two breakaway partners and took a healthy lead over the small group of favorites, from which Fausto Coppi and Louison Bobet broke clear. But Forestier did not falter. Exhausted but victorious, he finish 15 seconds in front of Coppi, who outsprinted Bobet for second place.

This success freed Forestier from any complexes, and in 1956 he proved his tactical decisiveness at the Tour of Flanders. Four hundred meters

The 1955 Paris-Roubaix (above) and the maillot jaune worn for two days in the 1957 Tour de France are Forestier's finest memories.

from the finish, while the stars watched each other from the corners of their eyes and prepared for a bruising sprint, the Lyon native attacked and headed to victory. The following year Forestier won the green jersey of points at the Tour de France, in which he also wore the *maillot jaune* for two days. For a glorious unknown—not too bad.

JEAN FORESTIER

Born: October 7, 1930, in Lyon, France
Palmarès: Paris-Roubaix 1955. Tour of Flanders 1956. Tour de Romandie 1954 and 1957. Critérium National 1957. Polymultipliée 1953. Green jersey of Tour de France 1957.

Felice Gimondi
Elegance Made the Racer

In 1958 Luciano Pezzi, the former lieutenant of Fausto Coppi, ended his racing career. Becoming a *directeur sportif,* he brought the Salvarani corporation into cycling sponsorship in 1964 and set out immediately in search of young talents. At an amateur race in Meldola his gaze quickly landed on a young man in a jersey bearing the colors of the Sedrina sports club from Bergamo. His name was Felice Gimondi. He finished in only third place, but Pezzi went to congratulate him. He spoke of the young rider's marvelous pedaling style, his calmness during the race, and his position on the bike—all supreme qualities that made great road racers. This former teammate of Coppi went straight to the point: He asked Gimondi to give his word that he would not sign a professional contract without informing him. The two men shook hands.

Pezzi's judgment was good. Several weeks later Gimondi won the Tour de l'Avenir—the amateurs' Tour de France—and so made himself a target of the top professional teams. As promised, though, he signed a contract with Salvarani. It was the end of the first chapter.

The following year, after several difficult months, the new professional started the Giro d'Italia. He handled himself remarkably well and finished third, two places behind his team leader, Vittorio Adorni, the winner. It was agreed that Gimondi's participation in stage races would go no further in 1965. There was no question of riding the Tour de France for a young racer not yet twenty-three years old; it would be too heavy a task. But events decided otherwise. When it came time for Salvarani to put together its team for the Tour de France, Pezzi was worried: Many riders were sick or injured. For him, there was only one solution: Make an appeal to Gimondi. Things were not so simple, though. The young Italian was reluctant, thinking he was not mature enough to face such a monument of cycling. He was afraid of being forced to quit along the way. But Pezzi was also a monument … of persuasion. Gimondi found himself at the start of the Tour in Cologne, Germany. Of course no one dared to put a penny on the performance of this still pimply young man.

The big favorite, in the absence of Jacques Anquetil, was none other than Raymond Poulidor. The Frenchman finally had a clear path to Paris. But Gimondi—the divine surprise—rose to the challenge. On the second day he slipped into a thirteen-man break to Roubaix and finished 1:19 ahead of the peloton and Poulidor. The next day at Rouen Gimondi won the stage, gaining another half-minute. He finished a close second to Poulidor in the time-trial stage at Châteaulin, limited his losses to 1:38 on Mont Ventoux, and then shattered Poulidor's illusions by winning the time trial up Mont Revard by 1:23. "No regrets," Poulidor admitted. "I was

defeated by a better man." Felice Gimondi never forgot that compliment. Winner of the Tour in his first season as a pro, followed by a win in Paris-Roubaix the following spring, Gimondi survived his intoxicating beginnings with distinction. When Eddy Merckx came charging up behind him, he immediately made the most courageous, difficult decision: He did all that was humanly possible to remain with the Cannibal, to assure himself of first place should his competitor happen to weaken. Gimondi reaped the fruits of this clever strategy, particularly at the 1973 world championship, on the Montjuich circuit in Barcelona. After escaping with Merckx, Freddy Maertens, and Luis Ocaña, Gimondi knew how to profit from the rivalry of the two Belgians, positioning himself on the wheel of one, then the other, and then seizing victory in the sprint. With his clever strategy and inherent talent, Gimondi managed to win everything that anyone could wish for.

FELICE GIMONDI

Born: September 29, 1942, in Sedrina, Italy
Palmarès: World Championship 1973. Tour de France 1965. Giro d'Italia 1967, 1969, and 1976. Vuelta a España 1968. Tour de Romandie 1969. Paris-Roubaix 1966. Paris-Brussels 1966 and 1976. Tour of Lombardy 1966 and 1973. Milan–San Remo 1974. Grand Prix des Nations 1967 and 1968.

Felice Gimondi was one of the greatest Italian racers, distinguished and exalted.

Walter
Godefroot
The Enemy of Merckx

He belonged to that race of cyclists, born in Flanders, who became masters in the art of cycling. A squat, stocky man, Walter Godefroot was first a gymnast. At age fifteen he was the school gymnastics champion in his Ghent region. He undoubtedly could have been successful in an entirely different discipline, but he was preoccupied with the bicycle, naturally enough, because there is no Flemish citizen who hasn't tried cycling at one time or another. Godefroot would go far in his chosen sport, but, without a doubt, his greatest misfortune was to belong to the same generation as Eddy Merckx, who was two years younger.

He was always Merckx's bugbear. In Tokyo, at the 1964 Olympic Games, Eddy and Walter mutually refused any sort of collaboration. Afterward each criticized the other for their collective failure. In 1965 they found themselves in the pro ranks at the same time. That first year Godefroot won the Belgian road championship, defeating Merckx by a wheel. Two years later he won Liège-Bastogne-Liège, then Paris-Roubaix in 1969, each time ahead of Merckx. Godefroot would also win the Tour of Flanders on two occasions, as he did Bordeaux-Paris.

Before long, however, the Merckx-Godefroot rivalry was strictly confined to the playing field. Over the course of the years the two men matured and learned to respect and appreciate each other. In the end Merckx could not scorn the loyalty and generosity of his blue-eyed countryman. Godefroot was, like Merckx, a man of combat, one who contributed to the structure of a race before thinking about how he could profit from it. He was the sprinter who battled with everything he had. What did it matter if, in him, a greyhound's speed gave way to a bulldog's strength?

At the start of his career he raced exclusively for himself. As he grew older, he learned to make concessions, to be less exclusive and less greedy. He knew when he could take a gamble on victory and when he could not, aware of his limits. In Paris-Roubaix, during his golden days, he was wild and unrestrained. He would not have offered his help to anyone. He concentrated essentially on his own race and on his potential victory. At other times, later in his career, he preferred to work for a teammate. Thus, in the 1978 Tour of Flanders, he agreed to work for Didi Thurau, a German colleague on his Ijsboerke team. The plan anticipated that Walter would slip into a breakaway, serving as a springboard for the young German. But Thurau was not equal to the task that day, and Godefroot had the last word, winning ten years after his first victory in the race.

That fall, after fourteen years as a pro, he decided to hang up his bike for good. Until the end you had to appreciate his sense of duty. Thus, at Tronchienne, as he was competing in his last kermesse race, he found himself in a breakaway with Roger De Vlaeminck after an intensive bout

of attacking. The two men were linked by a friendship established over the years. It was expected, evidently, that the Gypsy would offer this farewell race to the hero of the day. But Godefroot asked De Vlaeminck to contest the sprint honestly, and he lost. That day Godefroot was happier finishing second than if he had taken the victory as a gift. Right through his final race, he respected his profession.

Walter Godefroot was the symbolic Flemish racer—ready to give his all, always in the action, and never giving up.

WALTER GODEFROOT

Born: July 2, 1943, in Ghent, Belgium
Palmarès: Paris-Roubaix 1969. Bordeaux-Paris 1969 and 1976. Liège-Bastogne-Liège 1967. Tour of Flanders 1968 and 1978. Ghent-Wevelgem 1968. Championship of Zürich 1970 and 1974. Grand Prix of Frankfurt 1974. Four Days of Dunkirk 1974. Belgian Championship 1965 and 1972. Green jersey of Tour de France 1970.

Laurent
Jalabert
The Stakhanovite

In 1995 Laurent Jalabert crossed the greatest of hurdles: Already an excellent racer, he became the world's number-one-ranked rider. There had been no alternative. The first step of his metamorphosis took place that year at Paris-Nice—first of all on the second stage, with an unforeseen and victorious breakaway by a racer who we thought would never be more than a sprinter. Then, at the end of the race, we witnessed his dominance in the Col d'Èze time trial, to clinch the overall title.

Traditionally, Milan–San Remo follows Paris-Nice. Jalabert was there, and his sense of tactics and clarity of thought allowed him to benefit from the efforts already put in by his ONCE teammates Alex Zülle and Erik Breukink. Finally there was his fierce reaction to Maurizio Fondriest's devastating attack toward the summit of the Poggio and his masterful sprint down the Via Roma to beat the Italian star.

The Frenchman had just entered his seventh season as a professional, having already collected the green jersey of the Tour de France in 1992 and no fewer than seven stages at the previous year's Vuelta a España, including one in the high mountains.

Jalabert had made quite a comeback from his horrendous crash in the 1994 Tour de France. That accident happened in the mass sprint finish of the opening stage at Armentières, where he found himself on the ground, severely injured, along with several other riders, due to an on-duty gendarme inexplicably stepping into the street to take a photo instead of keeping order. Once he was fully recovered Jalabert wanted to prove himself in the grand tours, and especially the Tour de France, then the private domain of Miguel Indurain. At the 1995 Tour the Spaniard won the *maillot jaune* on the eighth stage. Five days later the fourteenth stage crossed the hills of the Forez, Velay, and Margeride to reach the heights above Mende, on the summit of its limestone plateau. The country, in the grip of a heat wave, was celebrating Bastille Day—the day chosen by Jalabert and his ONCE team to launch a fierce offensive against the race leader. When Jalabert launched his first attack at kilometer 25, several riders joined him, including his teammate Melchor Mauri and Italians Andrea Peron and Massimo Podenzana. Indurain didn't respond quickly enough, and by the time he had assembled his troops, he had already lost four minutes. When the gap passed the ten-minute mark on entering the Lozère region, Jalabert became the virtual race leader. A vigorous push by Indurain and his Banesto team cut the gap in half, but Jalabert, now alone, began the steep ascent at Mende to win the stage in dominant fashion. In Paris he was fourth overall and once again had the green jersey on his shoulders, to achieve his best Tour de France. Though he had not been able to win the *Grande Boucle,* he still had the Vuelta ahead of him. This

At age twenty-nine Laurent Jalabert became the champion of France, perhaps the least of his achievements.

time he would not be denied. Jalabert took the leader's yellow jersey at Alto del Naranco, a rocky peak that rises above the city of Oviedo and its factories. He won in every type of stage, five in all, as well as in the sprints, and walked away with every classification.

It would be difficult for him to do better in the following years, even though he won the world time trial championship in 1997 and remained at the top of the world rankings for another four seasons.

Jalabert went through a lot of torment after France was hit by doping scandals from 1998 onward, and he refused to accept the notion that accused racers should be "treated like cattle." He wanted nothing to do with France—this champion in the French tricolor jersey—but he returned at the start of 2000 to prove, on his bike, that he certainly deserved his title of the number-one racer in the world.

LAURENT JALABERT

Born: November 30, 1968, in Mazamet, France
Palmarès: World Time Trial Championship 1997. Vuelta a España 1995. French Championship 1998. Tour of Lombardy 1997. Milan–San Remo 1995. Clasica San Sebastian 2001. Flèche Wallonne 1995 and 1997. Classique des Alpes 1996 and 1998. Milan-Turin 1997. Paris-Nice 1995, 1996, and 1997. Critérium International 1997. Midi Libre 1996. Tour of the Basque Country 1999. Green jersey of Tour de France 1992 and 1995. Best climber of Tour de France 2001.

Jan Janssen
The Low Countries at the Top

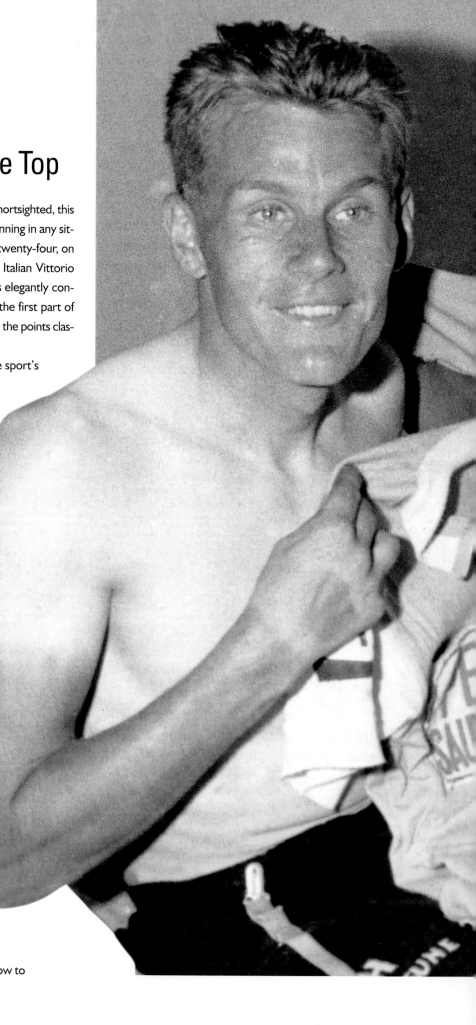

He was the archetype of the true professional. Though shortsighted, this bespectacled rider saw far ahead and was capable of winning in any situation. Jan Janssen became the world champion at age twenty-four, on the Sallanches circuit in the French Alps, ahead of the Italian Vittorio Adorni and the Frenchman Raymond Poulidor. He thus elegantly confirmed the promising words written about him during the first part of that 1964 season, which saw him win Paris-Nice and take the points classification at the Tour de France.

In two years as a pro cyclist Janssen had climbed to the sport's highest levels. Cycling, for which he had practically given up his adolescent passion of speed skating, generously returned to him what he put into it. For this Dutchman was already what, in the cycling world, we would call with admiration a "racer"—that is to say, an attacker rather than a man who spends his days following the wheels of others. At age fifteen he received his first racing bike as a reward for brilliant results in his school exams that would allow him to attend the technical school in The Hague. Three years later, somewhat forgetting his studies, Janssen began racing and won his first noteworthy victory: the Munstergelen Prize. Many more would follow.

In 1964, a paradox. A man from the Low Countries was crowned world champion in the most mountainous region of France, at Sallanches. On that rainy day in the Alps the uncertainties of the championship were simple enough: It wasn't known who would emerge from the pack, but it soon became apparent that two-time champion Rik Van Looy wouldn't be in the running for another victory. Janssen proved that he was one of the strongest and that he had the strength to win the rainbow jersey. Poulidor realized this when he couldn't drop the Dutchman on the last climb up to the village of Passy. In the final sprint Janssen put one bike length into Adorni, and more into Poulidor. Both a sprinter and a time trialist, the Dutchman knew how to

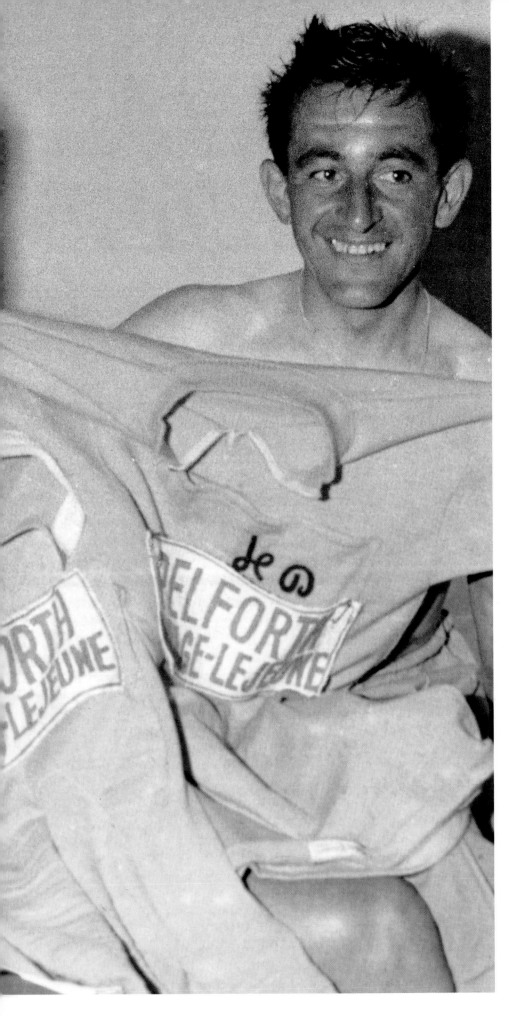

suffer. Soon his rivals began to respect his climbing abilities in the high mountains, where his regularity was stunning. Already in 1966 he might have won the Tour de France if a certain Lucien Aimar had not ambushed the race on the road to Turin.

Janssen's turn came two years later, at the eleventh hour, in the final stage time trial from Melun to Paris. Going into the stage, nine riders were within 2:30 of each other, such was the extraordinary suspense produced by a Tour that proved to be one of the most unusual in the postwar period.

"In the morning," Janssen remembers, "I was third in the general classification, 16 seconds behind the Belgian Herman Van Springel. We had ridden a first half-stage, where I had made very few efforts. Everything would be decided in the afternoon. I was ready, sure, but I had never competed in such a long time trial [55.2 kilometers]. Van Springel was the favorite to win, being a time-trial specialist. But I wanted to give everything I had. After 3 kilometers I already had a 15-second lead over the Belgian. I realized that I was about to win the Tour de France. When I watched Van Springel come onto the track [at the finish], he seemed to be off his stride. I knew then that I had won." Janssen's Tour de France victory was the first by a rider from the Netherlands.

Tour de France 1964: Jan Janssen poses with his green jersey, alongside his teammate Georges Groussard, the temporary maillot jaune.

JAN JANSSEN

Born: May 19, 1940, in Nootdorp, the Netherlands
Palmarès: World Championship 1964. Tour de France 1968 (second in 1966). Vuelta a España 1967. Paris-Roubaix 1967. Bordeaux-Paris 1966. Paris-Nice 1964. Paris-Luxembourg 1967. Championship of Zürich 1962. Green jersey of the Tour de France in 1964, 1965, and 1967.

Hennie Kuiper
Style and Method

Hennie Kuiper undoubtedly did not receive all the recognition he deserved. It is a fact that in the history of cycling we too often forget the unassuming men—those who, after crossing the finish line, do not make controversial remarks or use revenge-filled words. Kuiper was a superb champion and a remarkable representative of his sport. He won the majority of his victories by making solo breakaways in the style of the great champions. He had a head start when he won the road-racing gold medal at the 1972 Olympics in Munich. Three years later he was no less than the world professional champion, in Yvoir, Belgium—which made him the only rider besides Ercole Baldini to win both the world and Olympic road titles.

Kuiper also handled himself remarkably well in stage racing, even though second places, in the Tour de France as in other races, rarely leave a mark on history. In his defense, he did not always receive the respect he deserved. Second at the 1977 Tour, only 48 seconds behind Bernard Thévenet, he fell victim to the decision of his *directeur sportif,* Peter Post, to defend at all costs the *maillot jaune* of their TI-Raleigh team's German rider Didi Thurau. Then in 1978, after being declared the winner of the Alpe d'Huez stage after the disqualification of Michel Pollentier, Kuiper was the victim of a fall on the next stage and was forced to quit the race.

But Kuiper took his revenge in the classics, merging style with method. He who had long appeared to be exclusively a stage racer, for lack of a good sprint, nevertheless created an enviable palmarès, highlighted by victories in Paris-Roubaix, the Tour of Flanders, the Tour of Lombardy, and Milan–San Remo. They were all victories achieved with panache and by not giving a chance to the sprinters. He was never afraid, no matter who the opponent. If he had not been this way, he would never have built such a prestigious place for himself among the peloton's strongmen. As an athlete he never stopped fighting and always had the heart to place the work itself far above the job to be done. Above all, he always believed in his destiny. As strange as it may seem, his victories were, as a general rule, a response to an injustice or a profound disappointment. Throughout his career he often made the mistake of thinking too much about others and not enough about his own chances. But life needed to teach him to say "no" in certain cases.

In October 1978 he attended a seminar in Antwerp called Leading Success People (LSP). With these three initials he formed a motto in his native Dutch—*"Leef steeds positief"*—which translates as "Always have a positive outlook on life." Though on this occasion he was closed up in a hotel all weekend, it was because he wanted to give a new meaning to his life. When he arrived at the seminar he was asked, "What do you expect from your stay with us?" Without hesitation he answered, "That you help me win the Tour de France." At the end of this therapy he was convinced that victory could not escape him in the 1979 Tour. We know that he didn't win. But he came close, finding himself at one point only 30 seconds behind the eventual winner, Bernard Hinault. If bad luck had not befallen his team during the team time trial stage and left them with five punctures, he undoubtedly would have put the *maillot jaune* on his shoulders for the first time in his career.

HENNIE KUIPER

Born: February 3, 1949, in Denekamp, Netherlands
Palmarès: World Championship 1975. Olympic Road-Race Champion 1972. Paris-Roubaix 1983. Milan–San Remo 1985. Tour of Lombardy 1981. Tour of Flanders 1981. Tour of Switzerland 1976. Dutch Championship 1975.

Kuiper twice placed second at the Tour de France, and for the completeness of his career he deserved at least one maillot jaune.

Marc
Madiot
Smooth and Stylish

Spotted by the *directeur sportif* Cyrille Guimard when he was winning races in the amateur ranks, Marc Madiot made his first breakthrough when he won the amateur version of Paris-Roubaix in 1979. As a professional he continued his progression alongside Renault team leader Bernard Hinault and also excelled in cyclo-cross, wearing the French champion's jersey as early as 1982. Two years later he took victories in the Polymultipliée, the Flèche Finistérienne, and the Louvroil stage of the Tour de France.

In 1985 his career took on an added dimension when he took a superb victory at Paris-Roubaix. That year the queen of the classics had seemed destined for a racer from the powerful Panasonic team, maybe Phil Anderson, Eric Vanderaerden, or Eddy Planckaert. Yet when Madiot, elegant and aggressive, attacked on the cloying cobblestones of a slightly uphill stretch at the Carrefour de l'Arbre, 14 kilometers from the finish, no one could join him. He seemed to be racing at a different level. Beneath his mask of black mud was an exceptional freshness, in contrast to the growing weariness of the chasers, headed by the defending champion, Sean Kelly, who seemed to be the strongest of them. Madiot made short work of all that had been laboriously constructed since the morning by Francesco Moser, Theo De Rooy, Silvano Contini, Gregor Braun, Vanderaerden, and even his own brother Yvon.

One might imagine that after this great result, Marc Madiot's progress wouldn't have stopped there. But that's what happened. A throbbing pain in his knee stopped his racing for a while, and then, at the start of the 1987 season, he crushed some ligaments in a crash at the Three Days of De Panne. He had a lot of trouble overcoming and defeating this handicap, but his perseverance was rewarded in June when, in the Beaujolais region of France, he won the French national road championship. Before the end of the season he also won the Tour de l'Avenir. Despite Madiot's successes, there had already been some disagreement between him and *directeur sportif* Guimard. The result was his leaving the team he had been with for eight years, and the man who had been his mentor since his professional debut. Madiot signed for the Toshiba team, but a three-year spell there didn't produce much for him.

Then, six years after his first victory in Paris-Roubaix, after moving to the Grenoble-based RMO team, he again started the cobblestone classic in ideal physical and psychological shape. He had prepared himself well, knew the race and its pitfalls, and

took care to never let his mind wander. On the eighteenth of the twenty-two cobblestone sections, Madiot made a winning move almost identical to the one he had made in 1985, this time pulling away from a group of nineteen in his smooth, stylish manner. The chase was eventually taken up by the Italian Franco Ballerini, but Madiot never looked back and continued increasing his lead to win by more than a minute.

Madiot capitalized on this victory with a move to the German squad, Telekom, then to the American team, Subaru-Montgomery, but he won no more significant victories, and he ended his racing career in 1994.

Marc Madiot's victory in the 1985 Paris-Roubaix (above) was the perfect illustration of his raw talent. Two years later he won the French champion's tricolor jersey (left page).

MARC MADIOT

Born: April 16, 1959, in Renazé, France
Palmarès: Paris-Roubaix 1985 and 1991. Grand Prix de Wallonie 1985. French Championship 1987. Tour de l'Avenir 1987. Polymultipliée 1984. French Cyclo-Cross Championship 1982.

Francesco
Moser
The Best of a Dynasty

He had an imposing stature for a bike racer: five-foot-eleven and 172 pounds. He had a natural elegance, as much in the saddle as in street clothes, and in his gaze burned the flame of a broodingly handsome man. Francesco Moser, born on June 19, 1951, to Ignazio and Cecilia Moser in Palù di Giovo, a mountain town near Trento, Italy, was the eighth of eleven children. He was born on the very day that the oldest, Aldo, who would later defeat Roger Rivière to win the Grand Prix des Nations, was competing in his first race. Papa Ignazio, a carpenter and farmer in his spare time, died before Francesco grew up. Aldo became the head of the family and honored his responsibilities by succeeding as a pro racer. Thanks to his efforts and those of a younger brother, Enzo, the Moser clan managed to survive. Francesco, unlike his oldest brother, did not have to race in order to support the family. Perhaps this is one of the reasons that he didn't become involved in cycling until the relatively late age of seventeen.

The young Moser—"Checco," as he was called—would move quickly through the ranks. As an amateur he won the national championship and the so-called Baby Giro d'Italia, and his move into pro racing was eagerly awaited. He put his supporters at ease in the spring of his second season, 1974, when at Paris-Roubaix he found himself in a breakaway with Roger De Vlaeminck that left everyone else, including Eddy Merckx, floundering. Watching the two leaders race side by side—Moser so at ease with the wind, rain, and cobblestones—one could have believed they were both Flemish. But the Italian crashed and had to content himself with second place. Even so, Moser's performance won him the attention, respect, and envy of his rivals.

But his career didn't take off as quickly as he hoped. He won a dozen semiclassics in Italy while accumulating an incredible series of second-

place finishes—most notably at the 1976 world championship in Ostuni, in southern Italy, where he lost to Freddy Maertens. However, Moser did not miss his chance the following year in San Cristobal, Venezuela. Displaying admirable physical freshness in the humid climate, he made quick work of the young German hopeful Didi Thurau in the final sprint. His career then took off, especially in 1978, after he won the first of three consecutive victories at Paris-Roubaix. The Giro d'Italia remained out of his reach, though....

Moser had just passed the thirty-year mark, and people said his pedaling was becoming labored. It was then that he developed a crazy project: to beat Merckx's "unbeatable" world hour record. The Italian put together an unprecedentedly experienced team of trainers, sports doctors, and technical consultants. A new, revolutionary bicycle with disc wheels, tested in secret, produced suspense mixed with distrust. Questions were also asked about his new training methods, recommended by his sports medical team, Professor Francesco Conconi and Dr. Enrico Arcelli. The day for the record attempt arrived, and Moser was on the start line at the velodrome of the University Sports Center in Mexico City—the same city but a different track than the one used by Merckx in 1972 to set his historic mark of 49.431 kilometers.

On January 19, 1984, Moser started his attempt to break the world records in the 5-, 10- and 20-kilometer distances, but it soon became clear that he would be able to continue for the full hour. Indeed, he

Didi Thurau, in the background, soon fell off the pace, and Moser won his third Paris-Roubaix in 1980 (above).

smashed Merckx's record, breaking the 50-kilometer barrier to end up with 50.808 kilometers. Four days later Moser returned to the track and broke his own record with a fabulous 51.151 kilometers.

That same year Moser went on to score two more stunning results—winning the Milan–San Remo classic in March and the Giro d'Italia in June. The circumstances of his victory over Laurent Fignon certainly favored the Italian—the Stelvio Pass, judged impassable by the race director, was bypassed. And in the final time-trial stage, the world-hour-record holder used his special "record model" bike to overcome a 90-second deficit on Fignon. Moser had completed his career.

FRANCESCO MOSER

Born: June 19, 1951, in Palù di Giovo, Italy
Palmarès: World Championship 1977. Italian Championship 1975, 1979, and 1981. Giro d'Italia 1984. Paris-Roubaix 1978, 1979, and 1980. Tour of Lombardy 1975 and 1978. Milan–San Remo 1984. Paris-Tours 1974. Championship of Zürich 1977. Flèche Wallonne 1977. Ghent-Wevelgem 1979. Giro del Lazio 1977, 1978, and 1984. Tour of Piedmont 1974. Tirreno-Adriatico 1980 and 1981. Midi Libre 1975. Baracchi Trophy 1974 (with Roy Schuiten), 1975 (with Gibi Baronchelli), 1979 (with Giuseppe Saronni), 1984 (with Bernard Hinault), and 1985 (with Hans-Henrik Oersted). World Hour Record 1984 (50.808 and 51.151 km).

Johan
Museeuw
Through Pain and Blood

What a rider, what a fighter, and what a finisher! Those qualities characterize this Flemish rider from the purest school of the great classics specialists. He has been described as kind, peaceful, and calm, with an unassuming personality, wanting to return to anonymity as soon as a race is over. Although there are a few classics missing from the palmarès of Johan Museeuw—notably the Italian monuments Milan–San Remo and the Tour of Lombardy—he proved to be a specialist in racing on cobblestones. Paris-Roubaix certainly smiled on him, starting in 1996, when he headed the powerful Mapei team. That year the Belgian revealed his winning intentions when he took his place at the start of the great French classic, so no one seemed surprised when he launched an early attack. He soon received the help of his teammates, the Italians Gianluca Bortolami and Andrea Tafi. Their joint breakaway would last for almost 100 kilometers across the worst cobblestones in the "Hell of the North," despite the efforts of their principal pursuers, Viatcheslav Ekimov, Andreï Tchmil, Stefano Zanini, and Franco Ballerini.

The three Mapei men sped toward Roubaix at 43.31 kilometers an hour, the second-best average ever achieved in the event. But which of the three teammates would win? Everyone expected an exciting sprint on the Roubaix velodrome. But the directors of Mapei, including the big boss, Giorgio Squinzi, decided that the victory would go to Museeuw. Squinzi called his *directeur sportif*, Patrick Lefévère, from his cell phone and gave his orders.

Selected for the Belgian team at the world championship later in the year, Museeuw initially wanted to decline the invitation. But Eddy Merckx, given the role of team manager, was able to find the words necessary to convince him to show up for the race in Lugano, Switzerland. The media gave him virtually no chance of winning on the hilly circuit. And Museeuw? Did he believe victory was possible when he broke away with the local Swiss rider, Mauro Gianetti? Well, he believed it was worth putting everything into their attack. They managed to stay clear of the chase pack, and the Belgian outsprinted the Swiss to don the rainbow jersey on his thirty-first birthday. By the end of the season he didn't know which jersey to sport—he was simultaneously the world champion, Belgian champion, and winner of the World Cup. But Johan Museeuw also built his palmarès through pain and blood. Paris-Roubaix, which had seen him in the winner's circle,

A festival for the Mapei team at the finish of Paris-Roubaix in 1996. Museeuw wins, ahead of Bortolami and Tafi.

next saw him lying in agony in the Forest of Wallers-Arenberg. Some loose, uneven cobblestones, the involuntary sideways swerve of a team-mate on an ancient stone shoulder, and Johan Museeuw found himself on the ground and unable to get up. His left knee was badly injured and became infected. Luckily, the danger of gangrene was avoided. The racer wondered whether he'd be able to continue his career, but the doctors only responded to his questions with more questions. A conservative prognosis was given. But he wouldn't leave it at that. At his own expense, Museeuw hired a kinesiologist and worked relentlessly each day. It took him four months to regain, little by little, the full range of motion in his knee. And four years passed before he won the "classic from hell" a second time. It was a victory that belonged to no one except Museeuw himself and his powerful Mapei armada that stifled the chase from behind—where the atmosphere was one of resignation mixed with admiration. After more than 40 kilometers on his own, Museeuw won

Paris-Roubaix again. As he crossed the finish line he lifted his once-wounded left leg to show the frenzied fans, who were entirely behind his cause. Two years later he repeated his feat, this time lifting ten digits to mark his tenth victory in a World Cup race. The surprising come-back owed nothing to chance in the life of this devilish Belgian.

JOHAN MUSEEUW

Born: October 13, 1965, in Varsenare, Belgium
Palmarès: World Championship 1996. Belgian Championship 1996. Paris-Roubaix 1996, 2000, and 2002. Tour of Flanders 1993, 1995, and 1998. Paris-Tours 1993. Championship of Zürich 1991 and 1995. Amstel Gold Race 1994. Het Volk 2000. Grand Prix Eddy Merckx 1995. Four Days of Dunkirk 1995 and 1997. Three Days of De Panne 1997. UCI World Cup 1995 and 1996.

Gastone
Nencini
The Lion of Tuscany

Gastone Nencini was at the level of some of his more illustrious prede-cessors, with notable victories in the Giro d'Italia (1957) and the Tour de France (1960). Among the Italians he also proved himself, along with Ercole Baldini, the champion of continuity—the unifying link between the heroic era of Bartali, Coppi, and Magni and that of another kind of cycling personified by Adorni, Gimondi, Motta, and Moser.

An excellent climber, the Florentine shone in the mountains, and his tech-nique, along with his audacity, allowed him to take great risks in the descents. One of his strong points was that he knew how to control races to perfection, and the great tours gave him the chance to prove it. Each time Nencini left his mark.

When he had been a pro for less than a year, in 1955, he seemed poised to win his first victory in the Giro d'Italia, wearing the leader's pink jer-sey until the next-to-last stage, Trento–San Pellegrino. His main chal-lenger, Fiorenzo Magni, had been secretly informed of some emergency roadwork, and he and Fausto Coppi united their efforts to crush the hopes of the rider from Tuscany. Nencini had to be content with third place overall.

Nencini would finally win the Giro in 1957, in a race that was the despair of Louison Bobet, who lost to the Italian by just 19 seconds. This

was the year when Charly Gaul stopped in the middle of the nineteenth stage to urinate; Louison Bobet and Raphaël Geminiani took advantage of the Luxembourger with a strong attack—and Gaul's pink jersey went to Nencini. Furious over his misadventure, Gaul then took Nencini's side in order to stop Bobet from winning.

Already that year Nencini had finished ninth at the Vuelta a España before going straight into the Giro—and winning. It's really a "no-no" to ride all three grand tours in the same year, but the Italian then went on to try his luck at the Tour de France. He didn't do so badly, winning two mountain stages, finishing sixth overall, and taking the King of the Mountains title—most notably being first over the mighty Galibier on his way to winning the Briançon stage.

Already the owner of a pink jersey, Nencini added the yellow in 1960. But winning the Tour was bittersweet because his task was made easier by Roger Rivière's dramatic crash on the Perjuret descent that ended the Frenchman's career. Before the accident Rivière was lying second over-all, 1:38 behind Nencini, but no one would deny that the Italian had been in a strong position to hold off his unfortunate rival.

The day before the finish of that 1960 Tour, July 16, race leader Nencini had the great honor of shaking hands with General de Gaulle, then pres-ident of the French republic, when the race made a brief stop at the pres-ident's home in Colombey-les-Deux-Églises. Nencini was visibly moved by the experience.

Five years later Nencini's career was ended by a serious fall on the descent of Barberini di Mugello, just a few steps from his home, during the Bologna-Sienna stage of the Menton-Rome race. It was a fate curi-ously similar to that of Rivière.

Nencini leads Anquetil up the Gavia Pass in the 1960 Giro d'Italia.

GASTONE NENCINI

Born: March 1, 1930, in Bilancino di Barberino, Italy
Died: February 1, 1980
Palmarès: Tour de France 1960. Giro d'Italia 1957. Three Varesine Valleys 1956.

Jan
Raas
The Science of Racing

Raas won the rainbow jersey before his home crowd in 1979 (right page).

JAN RAAS

Born: November 8, 1952, in Heinkenszand, Netherlands
Palmarès: World Championship 1979. Milan–San Remo 1977. Amstel Gold Race 1977, 1978, 1979, 1980, and 1982. Tour of Flanders 1979 and 1983. Paris-Tours 1978 (Blois-Montlhéry) and 1981 (Blois-Chaville). Paris-Roubaix 1982. Ghent-Wevelgem 1981. Paris-Brussels 1978. Het Volk 1981. Dutch Championship 1976 and 1983.

He was stubborn, courageous, and tough as nails, like all the inhabitants of Zeeland, the Dutch delta region of the Rhine and Schelde rivers. It was on the other side of the Netherlands, in the flowering Limburg, that he became the third Dutch rider in five years to win the world road championship. He triumphed in front of his own people, on the hilly Valkenburg circuit, on August 26, 1979. This rainbow champion was Jan Raas.

Few people knew then that he had just taken a dramatic revenge on fate. On the night of January 1 that year, the near-completed villa that he was having built caught fire. Only the ashen debris remained. For his wife, Anja, and two young children, Dany and John, Raas went back to work, pushing himself in training even harder than he had in the first four years of his pro career. The supreme result: He became the world champion. Many stories raced along with him that August day that were hardly to his honor. Raas was called a cheater when Dutch television cameras caught him in the peloton during the race taking a tow from one of his teammates on the Cauberg climb. We might also mention his lack of cooperation in the final breakaway.... But Raas dismissed all this with a single motion when it was brought up to him. His world title, he said, had not at all changed his way of thinking and acting.

Within his Raleigh team no one rider was favored, and the fact that a single leader was never designated allowed everyone to try his luck. With a high-caliber *directeur sportif* in Peter Post, the team knew that it existed first and foremost to win money and that if one man triumphed, each of his teammates would benefit from the victory.

Born in 1952, Jan Raas played soccer for his village team until he was fifteen. His passion for cycling was inspired by his brother-in-law, a former racer. He won the Dutch amateur road championship and turned pro in 1975. The victories came one after another: Milan–San Remo, Paris-Roubaix, the Tour of Flanders, four consecutive editions of the Amstel Gold Race, Paris-Tours, and Paris-Brussels, not to mention stage wins here and there, and even a *maillot jaune* at the Tour de France. A collector of prestigious victories, Raas seemed endowed with a sixth sense that could be called the science of racing. He had no equal, in fact, in the classics, for his ability to sway the course of events. On Team Raleigh he had discovered a vocation in which he took a sly pleasure—he was the invisible hand directing the others. Raas was the boss, the one who ran the operations, handed out the duties, and never hesitated to delegate power if the situation called for it. "I do not ride for second place," he said. That statement summarizes his philosophy quite well.

Stephen Roche
1987: The Radiant Year

A single season would have been enough to enter his name in the history books of cycling. The fantastic 1987 triple of this Dubliner, born in 1959, will remain in all our memories—the Giro d'Italia, Tour de France, and world championship. In the space of a few months he captured cycling's three most prestigious titles, the finest collection of victories that any budding racer could even dream to amass. Only one man had achieved such a triple before Roche, and he was the greatest of all: Eddy Merckx, in 1974.

Stephen Roche served his racing apprenticeship in France. At age twenty he landed by boat from Ireland at Le Havre and based himself in the Paris suburbs, racing for the Athletic Club of Boulogne-Billancourt—a sort of nursery club for professional teams. These were difficult beginnings, far from family and friends. But the young man did not lack guts, and success was not long in coming—prestigious victories such as the amateur Paris-Roubaix in 1980.

The young Irishman turned pro in 1981 and immediately made a dazzling breakthrough in the style of prodigal champions. In his first season he won Paris-Nice, the Tour of Corsica, the Tour de l'Indre-et-Loire, and Étoile des Espoirs and narrowly missed victory in the Grand Prix des Nations. Roche did not truly come into his own until 1985, with his victory in the two-day Critérium International and, especially, his third-place finish at the Tour de France, where he won a stage at the summit of the Col d'Aubisque after outclimbing Bernard Hinault, Greg LeMond, and the Colombian climbers. The powerful Italian team, Carrera, noticed him at

that point and gave him a big two-year contract. Unfortunately, a bad crash at the Paris six-day race that winter put things on hold. His knee was injured, and a throbbing pain took over. It was the beginning of a long ordeal. Doctors, physical therapists, masseuses, and quacks of every genre came, one after the other, to give their advice. At that point he had to resign himself to the idea of surgery.

But his suffering did come to an end, and he managed to finish the Tour de France in an uncharacteristic forty-eighth place. He was happy for the 1986 season to come to an end. The following year, 1987, would be his. He shot into action early. However, after leading Paris-Nice, he lost the race with a puncture on the last day, and at Liège-Bastogne-Liège, a gross tactical error cost him the win. His victory at the Tour de Romandie put him back on track before the Giro d'Italia—which he won despite major conflicts within his own team, particularly with teammate Roberto Visentini and the team director, Davide Boifava.

Roche had proven his supreme confidence at the Giro, and he then showed great courage at the Tour de France, fighting to the point of asphyxiation to counter the Spaniard Pedro Delgado on the alpine climb to La Plagne. From that moment he knew he would win the Tour—which he duly accomplished in the final time trial. He knew himself well. In an environment where so many racers can dominate on any given day, Roche was always consistent, equally good in time trials and on mountain climbs. And he was not afraid to suffer in order to win.

After his victorious Tour de France, worn out by a long tour of criteriums and obligatory social engagements, he arrived in Villach, in the Austrian Tyrol, for the world championship. He had no thoughts of victory, estimating that the circuit was too flat for him and would heavily favor the sprinters. With this in mind, he made a pact to put himself at the service of his Irish team colleague Sean Kelly without a second thought. Roche had judged correctly. The circuit's small hills weren't really selective, and the race sank into monotony. The sprinters, particularly Kelly and Italy's Moreno Argentin, were closely marking each other in the leading group as the race headed to the finish. With 400 meters to go, Roche pulled away superbly on the right side of the road. Behind him the rest looked at each other to find out who was going to sacrifice their chances to go after the Irishman. An instant of reflection, and it was too late. Roche held off Argentin by 10 meters to become the world champion. What a year!

In 1987 he was invincible: Stephen Roche leads here, ahead of Robert Millar and Roberto Visentini, during the Giro d'Italia (above).

STEPHEN ROCHE

Born: November 28, 1959, in Dublin, Ireland
Palmarès: Tour de France 1987. World Championship 1987. Giro d'Italia 1987. Paris-Nice 1981. Tour de Romandie 1983, 1984, and 1987. Critérium International 1985 and 1991. Four Days of Dunkirk 1980. Tour de l'Avenir 1987.

Andreï Tchmil
Horizons without Frontiers

The Soviet regime had not yet imploded when Andreï Tchmil moved to Italy with a band of aging Soviet amateur racers to form a new, underfinanced pro team called Alfa Lum, based in the tiny republic of San Marino. It proved a nightmare for the then twenty-six-year-old racer from the USSR and his colleagues because the Italian team directors knew that these athletes had crossed the point of no return and that the team's destiny was in their hands. The atmosphere became increasingly more suffocating. Tchmil, an intelligent guy, understood everything. He explored his options, and after two years with Alfa Lum (and only three top-three finishes in minor classics) an opportunity arose in the form of a modest contract with the Belgian team, SEFB. This was his first contact with Belgium, but it would not be the last. After gleaning four important wins in his year with SEFB, in 1992 he moved back to Italy, with its shimmering lights and Latin lifestyle that he couldn't forget. Tchmil signed with the GB-MG team of Mario Cipollini, Fabio

Baldato, and … Johan Museeuw, a Belgian. It may have been a better contract, but Tchmil was again stuck in the role of *domestique*—a role he had problems with. He knew he could do better on his own account. At that point the ex-Soviet sought to free himself from this new yoke. He wanted to be a free citizen and not a foreigner in the country where he lived. Italy was hardly the best choice for achieving this goal. Though he had come there in 1989, it had been not out of choice but simply to become a professional bike racer. The collapse of the Soviet Union had brought about identity troubles for Tchmil. He no longer knew where his home was. His various passports indicated first a Russian nationality, then Ukrainian, then Moldavian. He was subjected to much administrative harassment. In Italy, like most foreigners, he had to endure long waits in line to extend his residence visa. He also wanted to end his submissive role in the races. In 1994, at age thirty-one, he saw the chance for salvation in Belgium when the Lotto team *directeur sportif* Jean-Luc Vandenbroucke made him an interesting offer: to be the team's leader. He had reached his goal—it was now his turn to prove what he was worth.

The Belgian squad wasn't mistaken. Tchmil won Paris-Roubaix during his first year racing in Lotto red. And that was only the beginning. Soon he was appearing everywhere. In 1997 he became a Belgian citizen and straightened out his situation, which he had wanted to do for a long time. He made a home in this small country, won Paris-Tours that same year, and distinguished himself with stage victories in Paris-Nice.

Belgium adopted him. On the strength of his results he made his presence felt in virtually every major one-day race. What can we say about his victory in the 1999 Milan–San Remo? A stroke of genius. Within sight of the finish he attacked sharply, taking a good 20-meter lead. There were still 300 meters to go, but he managed to preserve his 20 meters with an effort of a rare intensity. A strong finisher had won, depriving Erik Zabel of a historic "threepeat."

From that moment on, Tchmil set his sights on the overall World Cup title, which he had almost won in 1994. He had the ability to compete on all types of terrain and in all kinds of weather in order to reach his ultimate goal. In fact, he scored points in all ten races, and this regularity allowed him to take control of the last few events—especially after placing third in the Championship of Zürich. Andreï Tchmil, this universal Belgian citizen, had won the World Cup of cycling. What a journey! The king of the Belgians was happy.

ANDREÏ TCHMIL

Born: January 22, 1963, in Khabarovsk, Russia
Palmarès: Paris-Roubaix 1994. Paris-Tours 1997. Milan–San Remo 1999. Tour of Flanders 2000. Grand Prix de Plouay 1994. Paris-Camembert 1995. Paris-Bourges 1991. Tour du Limousin 1995. UCI World Cup 1999.

For Tchmil the Lotto team certainly amounted to a whole lot!

Jan Ullrich
Iron Discipline

Jan Ullrich first learned strict training methods at the Dynamo Berlin sports school, which he entered in 1986 at the age of thirteen. There the secret of success began with iron discipline inculcated by the authoritarian Peter Becker, a controversial sports educator. Becker was both an adviser and a surrogate father to Jan, who was only nine when his father walked out on him and his mother.

Like all the students at the school, Ullrich, noted for his physical abilities, tried out many sports before being directed toward cycling after what Becker called "the hand test." The trainer examined the hand of each youth, taking special interest in the fingers and the joints, and determined the unique sport toward which the athlete-to-be should be oriented. The test certainly seems to have been reliable, for Jan Ullrich, after an easy passage into the cycling world, was successful in almost every discipline: track, cyclo-cross, and road. He even rose to the top of the amateur ranks, becoming the world road champion at Oslo in 1993. He was nineteen. Before the Berlin Wall came down in 1989, the teenage Ullrich had seen some videotapes of the Tour de France and had admired Laurent Fignon and Greg LeMond…. All in secret, of course. The Iron Curtain was still in place. In the reunified Germany the Telekom team was created in 1991, and by the time Ullrich was ready to turn pro it was the country's only international team. They wanted Ullrich because besides being talented, he was known to be loyal, with a perfect upbringing, and he would respect the team rules. These traits were perfectly illustrated at the 1996 Tour de France, two years after he joined Telekom. Ullrich went to his first Tour to learn his trade and to serve his team leader, Bjarne Riis of Denmark. He carried out this task to perfection. He was also called upon to show another facet of his talent late in the Tour, at the time-trial stage from Bordeaux to St. Émilion, a distance of 63.5 kilometers. Never had Ullrich raced solo over such a distance. Yet, after three weeks of efforts on the roads of France, this fine athlete, six feet one inch tall, averaged 50.443 kilometers per hour on his way to a prestigious stage win. Riis, his team captain and the *maillot jaune*, conceded more than two minutes to Ullrich. What a demonstration! He finished second in that Tour and seemed happy with his lot.

The following year, 1997, Ullrich stuck with the program and returned to the Tour de France to continue his apprenticeship and try to help Riis win again. He had a cold fear of being accused of betraying his leader. Therefore, when on stage nine's Val-Louron climb the Dane couldn't respond to the repeated attacks of the Festina team, Ullrich did not collaborate with the aggressors; he simply followed Festina's Richard Virenque and Laurent Brochard, controlling them. It was the work of a good teammate. Even though Riis conceded just half a minute that day, it was clear that he wasn't in the same state of grace as the previous year. He was in trouble again on the next stage, also in the Pyrenees. That was a signal for Ullrich to pick up the baton. He knew the rules:

Finish ahead of his friend, certainly, on the condition of not favoring a rival. Ten kilometers before the finish at the summit of Andorra-Arcalis, Ullrich accelerated and at that point decided to go for the stage win … though not the general classification. That was what teamwork decreed. A subtle difference, maybe…. Even so, the young German captured the *maillot jaune* and was now more than 4 minutes ahead of Riis. But then what? In the time-trial stage at St. Étienne, three days later, there was no longer any doubt that the final victory would go to Ullrich. He caught Virenque, who had started 3 minutes in front of him, while Riis too conceded 3 minutes. With the calm power that Ullrich displayed, his opponents certainly had much to fear. He could tackle the Alps with the greatest serenity. So at the age of twenty-three he became one of the youngest winners of the Tour de France. But glory is capricious. In spite of all the titles that he gathered here and there—notably in the Olympic road race and at the world time-trial championships—he has yet to regain the invincibility he demonstrated in 1997.

At the 1997 Tour Jan Ullrich was unstoppable, bringing the French public to its feet (above).

JAN ULLRICH

Born: December 2, 1973, in Rostock, (East) Germany
Palmarès: Tour de France 1997 (second in 1996, 1998, 2000, and 2001). Vuelta a España 1999. World Time-Trial Championship 1999 and 2001. Olympic Road Race Gold Medal 2000. German Championship 1997 and 2001.

Herman
Van Springel
Mr. Bordeaux-Paris

Herman Van Springel undoubtedly remains one of the most unrecognized racers in the history of cycling. Sure, he was later called Mr. Bordeaux-Paris because of his seven victories in that celebrated but now defunct French classic. But Van Springel's class was such that he certainly should have put together a more diversified palmarès than he did. This quiet Belgian undoubtedly lacked a little ambition. He turned up for races as if he were going to the factory. Perpetually sleepy, he had to be practically snapped out of his inertia when the race started. The gossips said that he went back to sleep during the race, going so far as to make the following joke: Van Springel won Bordeaux-Paris (whose average race time was between fourteen and fifteen hours) because it was the event in which he could sleep the longest. He was nevertheless a genuine champion who would certainly have won the 1968 Tour de France if he had truly believed in his chances. Wearing the *maillot jaune* going into the final stage, a time trial, Van Springel was surprisingly defeated by the Dutchman Jan Janssen and lost the Tour by 38 seconds. The image of the Belgian with his head hidden in his hands, crying hot tears, remains vivid in many memories. Though he was the winner of, notably, the Tour of Lombardy, Paris-Tours, and the Grand Prix des Nations, it was evident that Bordeaux-Paris was the favored event of the good Herman. In this ultramarathon race, in which the riders were motorpaced for the final few hours, he built a work of incomparable precision—an indivisible stamp of courage, persistence, talent, discipline, humility, health, and balance. Van Springel was all that, with the added trait of an engaging personality. He was a class act in the most noble, respected sense of the term.

He revealed that his preparations for Bordeaux-Paris were spread over fourteen days, with daily training rides of more than 400 kilometers, alternating sessions behind a motorcycle with solo efforts, all equally tedious. At age thirty-eight he won his seventh victory in what was called the Derby of the Road.

Van Springel wasn't what you'd call popular, hardly spectacular, but he was terribly effective. No *directeur sportif* could mold him, so carefully did he cultivate his independent character. But his other virtues kept him, from year to year, at the highest level. All the same, a more engaging smile, a touch more craftiness, would have allowed him to cross the boundary that separates the champion from the star. But did he want that?

Van Springel never laughed or smiled … except when he won.

HERMAN VAN SPRINGEL

Born: August 14, 1943, in Ranst, Belgium
Palmarès: Bordeaux-Paris 1970, 1974, 1975, 1977, 1978, 1980, and 1981. Tour of Lombardy 1968. Paris-Tours 1969. Championship of Zürich 1971. Ghent-Wevelgem 1966. Het Volk 1968. Grand Prix des Nations 1969 and 1970. Belgian Championship 1971. Baracchi Trophy 1969 (with Joaquim Agostinho). Second in Tour de France 1968. Green jersey of Tour de France 1973.

Index

PHOTO CREDITS

Printed in Spain